Cooking with Trader Joe's®

Cookbook

Gluten-Free

Deana Gunn & Wona Minati

Cooking with Trader Joe's Cookbook: Gluten-Free
by Deana Gunn and Wona Miniati
Photographs by Deana Gunn and Wona Miniati
Designed by Lilla Hangay
Produced by Deana Gunn and Wona Miniati

Published by Brown Bag Publishers, LLC
P.O. Box 235065
Encinitas, CA 92023
info@cookTJ.com

Printed in China through Overseas Printing Corporation

Library of Congress Cataloging-in-Publication Data
Gunn, Deana and Miniati, Wona
Cooking with Trader Joe's Cookbook: Gluten-Free/
by Deana Gunn and Wona Miniati; photographs by Deana Gunn and Wona Miniati – 1st ed.
Includes index.

I. Quick and easy cookery. 2. Trader Joe's (Store) I. Title.

ISBN   978-1-938706-02-8   1938706021

Table of Contents

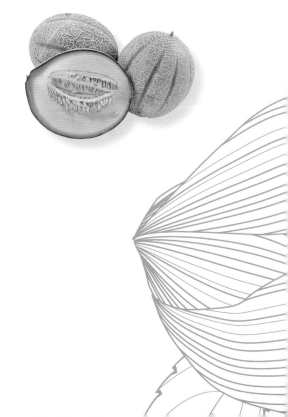

Thank You Notes

A heartfelt thanks to our family and friends who continue to cheer us on as we enthusiastically create more cookbooks starring our favorite store.

We praise our talented designer Lilla Hangay for making each book more beautiful and fun than the one before. We also thank our editor Heather World for polishing our prose and helping us say all them thar words in the goodest way.

Many thanks to our customers who share their feedback and favorite recipes with us. We love hearing from you, and your kind emails and calls make our day. In fact, you are the inspiration behind this cookbook. You asked for our best gluten-free recipes all in one place, and here they are (with a few new recipes added in)!

A big shout-out to Trader Joe's, our favorite store in the whole wide world. We can't imagine a better place to shop or nicer crewmembers to greet us as we cruise the aisles.

We thank you all!

Introduction

Years ago, we had the idea to create something new: a Trader Joe's cookbook. It was the perfect way to share all our original recipes and cooking ideas that helped us create meals easily and quickly every night of the week. The idea was simple: make Trader Joe's our one-stop shop and use their time-saving products in our recipes. For years, we had shopped the aisles, created recipes around what we saw, stocked up on our favorite products, and fantasized about how to use new products. We strategized about all the shortcuts that would cut our cooking time in a fraction of what it would be if we did everything the old-fashioned, from-scratch way. The cookbook was a resounding hit, because it turns out that we weren't the only ones looking for delicious, easy meals made in a snap.

A Gluten-Free Trader Joe's Cookbook

The gluten-free diet has become more popular in recent years, so it was no surprise when we started getting a growing number of requests for a gluten-free collection of Trader Joe's recipes. Deana's husband has been gluten free for years, so we were no strangers to the requirements and challenges of gluten-free eating. We began to assemble a collection of our favorite recipes that were inherently gluten free, like veggie curry and coq au vin, and added recipes that were created to fill a void left by the restrictions of a gluten-free diet, like gluten-free almond pie crust and gluten-free bread pudding. Thus was born a gluten-free cookbook for the Trader Joe's shopper—a cookbook that won't leave you skipping recipes or wondering how you can modify the ingredients to work around a recipe. Most of these recipes are collected from the other cookbooks in our series, though some have been created especially for this book.

Why Gluten Free?

Gluten is found in three foods: wheat, barley and rye. Gluten is the "glue" of certain foods and recipes: it's what gives breads, muffins, and pasta a chewy texture. A diet without gluten centers on meat, grains like quinoa and rice, beans and legumes, fruits and vegetables. For many people, it also includes substitutions for gluten-containing foods such as bread, pizza, pasta, and baked goods made from alternative flours such as rice, corn, almond, or coconut flour, just to name a few.

Gluten-free eating has soared in popularity over the last few years, primarily for three reasons:

1. People are learning they are allergic or sensitive to gluten. Symptoms may include mal-absorption of food, digestive issues, rashes, and low energy or fatigue. With some people, the reaction may be mild or may be aggravated by too much gluten. Others may have Celiac disease, an autoimmune reaction to gluten that can cause severe damage to the small intestine.

2. People are discovering that eliminating certain foods with gluten helps them lose weight and maintain it more easily. In a way, you're forced to eat healthier because a gluten-free diet eliminates a lot of processed junk food, breaded fried foods, high-carb breads and pastas, and many fattening and high-sugar desserts such as pie and pastries. Furthermore, wheat products are high-glycemic-index foods— foods that spike your blood sugar and create food cravings that can be confused with hunger. Get rid of them and you often get rid of the drive to overeat or eat impulsively. When eating gluten free, be wary of over-using gluten-free breads and pastas made from refined gluten-free flours and starches (rice, potato, corn, etc.) that can also have a high glycemic index.

3. Eliminating gluten can have other direct and indirect health benefits, such as improved cholesterol levels, improved cardiac health and reduced risk of cancers and diabetes.

Please note that products at Trader Joe's may be labeled "no gluten ingredients used" as opposed to the stricter "gluten-free." Even if a product was made with no gluten ingredients used, there is a risk it will may be contaminated with gluten if it is produced in a facility that handles products with gluten, such as wheat.

Persons with Celiac disease or severe gluten allergies should note that unless a product is certified gluten-free (per tests such as the ELISA gluten assay test) and produced in a dedicated facility, there is possibility of this cross-contamination.

As of this writing, there is no labeling regulation or standard threshold for gluten content or universal diet guidelines for those with Celiac disease. Always read labels and check for gluten content, even in products you use regularly, as ingredients may change. The Trader Joe's website lets consumers know that in its brand-name products, ingredients listed as "natural flavors" or "spices" do not contain gluten or gluten derivatives.

Our aim is not to convince you of whether or why you should eat gluten free. You and your doctor are the best judge of that. Our aim is to provide delicious recipes that are free of gluten ingredients and can be made easily, in minutes, with a simple trip to Trader Joe's.

Why Trader Joe's?

We are always surprised when we run into someone who's never shopped at Trader Joe's, because we can't imagine life without it! Ask someone what they love most about Trader Joe's, and you'll likely hear some of these reasons:

- **Value and quality.** At Trader Joe's, you'll find everything from the very basics to high-end gourmet food at affordable prices. All the food is high quality and delicious, with organic and natural options found throughout the store.

- **Unique products.** Trader Joe's scouts the world for new and inspiring foods and beverages. Only those that pass Trader Joe's employee taste tests make it to stores.

- **Just food, no preservatives.** When you compare the labels on Trader Joe's products to items found at other stores, you'll notice something missing: a long list of chemicals, fillers, and preservatives.

- **No artificial flavors and no artificial colors.** Whether it's the "pink" in pink lemonade or the colorful candy coating on the Chocolate Sunflower Seed Drops, the colorings are natural (usually vegetable extracts) rather than synthetic food dyes. Flavorings are also natural, which not only taste better but are healthier.

- **Nothing genetically engineered.** Trader Joe's was among the first national grocers to remove genetically modified food from its private label products.

- **Eco-conscious.** Trader Joe's is regularly recognized for its commitment to responsible buying practices. Trader Joe's brand eggs are cage-free. Hormone-free dairy products are the norm. Tuna is from "dolphin-safe" water (and as a result, low in mercury).

- **Wine and beer.** In addition to great food, Trader Joe's brings a wide and ever-evolving assortment of value-priced wines from all over the globe, including the famously nicknamed "Two-Buck Chuck." Trader Joe's international beer selection is second to none.

- **Fun-filled shopping experience.** Balloons, hand-written chalkboard signs, lively music, and cheerful crewmembers decked in Hawaiian flair create a friendly and casual atmosphere.

- **Gluten-free product listing.** Take a look at Trader Joe's website and you'll see a pretty comprehensive list of gluten-free products available at the store. As you shop, you will also see a gluten-free icon on many packages of Trader Joe's gluten-free products. Check labels because not all gluten-free products carry the icon.

So head on down to your nearest Trader Joe's with this cookbook in hand, and let us show you why this is our favorite grocer and our favorite way to cook.

About our recipes and this book

Our recipes are gluten free and fuss free. We have included:

1. Photos for every recipe.
We love cookbooks with photos. How else will you know if you'll like a recipe or what it will look like when it's done? We think it's necessary to have pictures with recipes, so we're continuing our tradition of giving you a photo of every single dish, made by us, in our own kitchens.

2. One-stop shopping at Trader Joe's.
We're too busy to run around from store to store, gathering ingredients. And we know you are, too. The recipes in this book are built on one-stop shopping: get everything you need at Trader Joe's and then get ready for the easiest cooking you can imagine. Throughout the book, we've capitalized the names of unique Trader Joe's products, such as Fresh Bruschetta Sauce or Chunky Salsa. Of course, it's not a *requirement* to get everything at Trader Joe's, but it's a convenience we invite you to embrace. And yes, we recognize that occasionally an item will be out of stock or (heaven forbid!) discontinued. That's why we suggest substitutions in each recipe and keep a running list of substitutions on our website, **cookingwithtraderjoes.com.**

3. Nutritional information.
A team of certified dietitians and nutritionists has evaluated each recipe, and nutritional data is given so you can match menus to your dietary needs. Whether you're interested in carbs, calories, or fat, whether you follow popular diets or have your own regimen, we hope the nutritional data provided in this book will help you create healthy menus.

Nutritional analysis for recipes assumes 1% milk, low-fat yogurt, and low-sodium broth unless otherwise noted. It does not include optional ingredients.

We note recipes that can be made vegetarian using simple substitutions.

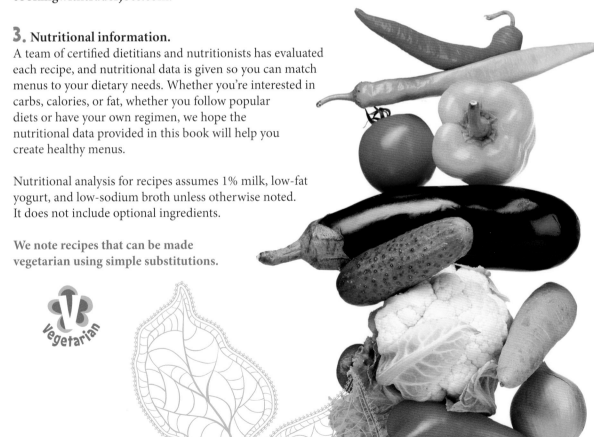

Kitchen Staples

Stock your kitchen with strategic basics, and you will have the foundation to create meals quickly. Below are some favorite Trader Joe's staples, including helpful gluten-free alternative products, to keep on hand. It's easy to combine them with vegetables, greens, meats, and other fresh ingredients to make mealtime a snap.

Pantry

- Extra virgin olive oil
- Balsamic or your favorite vinegar
- Vegetable, chicken, or beef broth (available gluten-free, in 32-oz cartons)
- Salsa
- Tamari or wheat-free soy sauce, gluten-free teriyaki sauce
- Olives, marinated artichokes, or roasted red peppers
- Sun dried tomatoes
- Canned beans
- Canned tomatoes
- Bruschetta, pesto, tapenade, or chutney
- Peanut butter, almond butter, or other nut butter
- Trail Mix and Nuts (these can be stored in the freezer if they are not used quickly)
- Almond meal (for baking or as a substitute for bread crumbs)
- Brown rice tortillas and corn tortillas
- Corn pasta or brown rice pasta
- Gluten-free granola
- Gluten-free bread and bagels (we like Udi's brand)
- Gluten-free rolled oats
- Dressing

Freezer

- Frozen Brown Rice or Jasmine Rice (packaged as 2-cup pouches in a box)
- Frozen Crushed Garlic (packaged as frozen cubes)
- Frozen mangoes, berries, or other frozen fruit
- Frozen vegetables such as broccoli, peas, spinach, and green beans
- Chicken, beef, fish, shrimp, or scallops. Chicken, salmon, and steaks are often sold in separately packaged freezer-safe bags, or you can separate them into individual portions before freezing.
- Frozen boxed appetizer for unexpected guests (such as Mini Chicken Tacos)
- Frozen gluten-free pancakes and toaster waffles for those rushed mornings
- Pre-made foods such as frozen tamales or Chili Lime Chicken Burgers

Spice Cabinet

- Basil
- Oregano
- Rosemary
- Cumin
- Cinnamon
- Curry powder
- Vanilla extract
- Nutmeg
- Salt and pepper (available with convenient built-in grinders)
- 21 Seasoning Salute, an all-purpose sodium-free blend of herbs and spices

Conversions

Volume Measurements

3 teaspoons   = 1 tablespoon
4 tablespoons   = ¼ cup
16 tablespoons   = 1 cup
2 cups   = 1 pint
2 pints   = 1 quart
4 quarts   = 1 gallon

2 tablespoons   = 1 fluid ounce
1 cup   = 8 fluid ounces

Weight Measurements

16 ounces = 1 pound

Abbreviations

tsp   = teaspoon
Tbsp = tablespoon
oz   = ounce
lb   = pound
pkg   = package

Eyeballing Measurements

Most recipes don't require painstaking measurement unless you're baking. Ingredients can usually be eyeballed.

An easy way to eyeball cup measurements is to think of the volume of an average apple. That's about a cup. Half an apple is about half a cup. The volume of an egg is about ⅓ cup.

Pour a tablespoon of olive oil in your pan and see what it looks like in the pan. Once you get a feel for what it looks like, just eyeball it from then on.

Pour a teaspoon of salt in the palm of your hand. After you see that a few times, trust your eye as the judge.

Appetizers

Flax Seed Crackers

These crackers are crunchy and full of gluten-free, no-carb goodness. Flax seeds are a great source of fiber, phytochemicals, lignans, and healthy essential fatty acids. Serve with any kind of cheese, dip, nut butter, or solo as a snack. Roasted flax seeds have a nutty flavor, which some liken to roasted seaweed. Conversely to what many think, conventional roasting is not found to destroy the nutritional benefits of flax seeds. Raw flax seeds have a milder flavor and chewier texture but work just as well with this recipe. They will take longer to dry out in the oven, so leave them overnight.

2 cups whole roasted flax seeds (tap measuring cup to settle contents)
2 cups water
1 tsp salt

1 Combine flax seeds, water, and salt in a large bowl and let sit for 15 minutes. The mixture will become very thick and gelatinous.

2 Preheat oven to 150° F. Line two standard 12x17-inch baking sheets with foil and lightly oil with vegetable oil or use a silicone baking mat (no oil necessary).

3 Place half of the mixture on each sheet. Wet your hands and use them to press and spread the mixture very flat and evenly across the entire sheet.

4 Place in oven and heat for 6 hours (or overnight up to 8 hours). The crackers will be dried out and crisp. If not, return to oven until they are completely dry. Peel off foil if it adheres.

5 Let crackers cool, break apart into smaller cracker-size pieces, and store in plastic bag or airtight container.

Variations: *Once you try this basic recipe, make flavored crackers. Add garlic and herbs, cinnamon and sugar, or substitute 2 Tbsp tamari for the salt.*

Prep time: *5 minutes (not counting soaking time)*
Hands-off cooking time: *6 hours up to overnight*
Serves *16*

Nutrition Snapshot
Per serving: 90 calories, 7g fat, 1g saturated fat, 3g protein, 4g carbs, 4g fiber, 0g sugar, 125mg sodium

Note: *Chew flax seeds well to get the most health benefits! Chewing gets out the valuable oils and phytochemicals.*

Tip: *If your oven does not go as low as 150° F, you will need to watch them closely over a shorter baking time or use a dehydrator instead.*

Warm Honeyed Figs with Goat Cheese

When figs are in season, enjoy the classic combination of sweet ripe figs and tangy goat cheese as an appetizer or even as dessert. Fresh figs spoil quickly, so plan on using them within a day or so.

. . . .

12 medium or large fresh figs
1 tsp extra virgin olive oil
1 Tbsp honey
2 oz goat cheese

1 Cut each fig in half, from stem to end.
2 Heat olive oil in a skillet over medium heat. Place figs in skillet cut side down and sauté for 1-2 minutes until faces are hot and slightly caramelized. Remove from heat.
3 Drizzle figs with honey and gently toss to distribute honey.
4 Place figs face up on a platter. Place a few crumbles of goat cheese in the center of each fig. Goat cheese will soften slightly from the heat of the figs. Serve immediately.

Variation: *Substitute mascarpone for goat cheese. Or wrap prosciutto around the fig/cheese combination and enjoy a taste explosion!*

Prep and cooking time: *10 minutes*
Serves *6 (4 pieces per serving)*

Nutrition Snapshot
Per serving: 146 calories, 4 g fat, 2 g saturated fat, 3 g protein, 28 g carbs, 4 g fiber, 24 g sugar, 35 mg sodium

Note: *If using very small figs, cut off tops, slice down into tops just a little, sauté, and stuff with goat cheese.*

Prosciutto-Wrapped Scallops

Prosciutto cooks up crisp in the oven and is a nice balance to the soft scallops. Serve these tasty morsels as an appetizer or as an elegant dinner served on a bed of salad or quinoa.

. . . .

    1 lb jumbo scallops, thawed if frozen (about a dozen scallops)

    6 slices prosciutto, cut lengthwise in half, or bacon may be substituted

    2 Tbsp Green Olive Tapenade, or any tapenade or bruschetta you like

1 Preheat oven to 375° F.

2 Lightly pat scallops dry with a clean paper towel. Season scallops with the tapenade, making sure to coat all sides evenly.

3 Wrap each scallop with a band of prosciutto. Place seam side down in a buttered baking dish or cookie sheet. Spread scallops 2 inches apart so that they roast and don't steam.

4 Bake for 15-16 minutes. Do not overcook. Scallops are done when they are opaque and no longer translucent.

Prep time: *10 minutes*

Hands-off cooking time: *15-16 minutes*

Serves *4 (about 3 scallops each)*

Nutrition Snapshot

Per serving: 318 calories, 15 g fat, 3 g saturated fat, 6 g protein, 35 g carbs, 4 g fiber, 11 g sugar, 963 mg sodium

Breezy Caprese Salad

This informal version of the classic Italian salad is fresh as spring. Colorful heirloom tomatoes are especially wonderful here, but any ripe tomatoes will do. Creamy fresh mozzarella is conveniently pre-sliced and ready when you are.

· ·

3 tomatoes, cut in thick slices

1 (8-oz) container Fresh Mozzarella Medallions, or slice your own

1 bunch basil leaves

2 Tbsp extra virgin olive oil

Pinch salt and pepper

1 Arrange tomato slices and cheese medallions on a simple platter. Tuck basil leaves between tomatoes and cheese.

2 Drizzle platter liberally with olive oil. Sprinkle generously with salt and pepper.

Prep time: *5 minutes*
Serves *4*

Nutrition Snapshot
Per serving: 207 calories, 16 g fat, 6 g saturated fat, 13 g protein, 6 g carbs, 2 g fiber, 4 g sugar, 202 mg sodium

Herb Goat Cheese Log

How do you take fresh goat cheese from simple to sublime, from plain to pretty? Roll a goat cheese log in fresh chopped herbs, nuts, and berries to complement its tangy taste and creamy texture. Serve with rice crackers, endive leaves, or apple slices. Crumble leftovers on top of greens to make an extra special salad.

· ·

> 1 (8-oz) log Chevre goat cheese, plain (larger size is okay)
> ½ cup chopped and crushed Candied Pecans or other nuts
> ½ cup chopped fresh basil
> ½ cup chopped dried cranberries
> ¼ tsp black pepper

1 Combine pecans, basil, cranberries, and pepper on plastic wrap.
2 Unwrap goat cheese log and place in nut mixture, using plastic wrap to roll and press cheese log firmly in the mixture. Once the cheese log is fully coated, wrap in the plastic wrap and chill until ready to serve.

Prep time: *5 minutes*
Serves *6*

Nutrition Snapshot
Per serving: 207 calories, 14 g fat, 6 g saturated fat, 8 g protein, 12 g carbs, 2 g fiber, 10 g sugar, 90 mg sodium

Hello Portobello!

Portobello (or Portabella) mushrooms are earthy and meaty, making them popular in many vegetarian dishes. Here, we top each mouthwatering cap with cheese, tangy sun dried tomatoes, and delicate micro greens, all served on a bed of mixed salad.

. . . .

2 Portobello mushroom caps, stems removed

Pinch salt

2 slices Havarti cheese

1 Tbsp Julienne Sliced Sun Dried Tomatoes, drained, and 1 Tbsp oil from jar

1 tsp finely chopped fresh basil, or 1 cube Frozen Basil

1 (5-oz) bag Organic Baby Spring Mix, or 3 cups of other salad mix

2 cup Organic Micro Greens

1 Preheat oven to 400° F.

2 Place Portobello caps gill-side up on a lightly oiled baking sheet. Sprinkle each with salt.

3 Bake for 10 minutes. During the last 2 minutes, add cheese on top and sprinkle on sun dried tomatoes. Remove from oven. Don't worry if Portobellos don't seem quite done. They will continue to cook and will become very juicy in minutes.

4 Place a big handful of salad mix on each plate and place one Portobello cap on top. Top each cap with micro greens.

5 Mix together oil and basil and drizzle on top of each cap and salad.

Prep time: *5 minutes*
Hands-off cooking time: *10 minutes*
Serves *2*

Nutrition Snapshot
Per serving: 227 calories, 10 g fat, 7 g saturated fat, 11 g protein, 10 g carbs, 4 g fiber, 1 g sugar, 268 mg sodium

Polenta Rounds with Mushrooms

Pre-cooked polenta logs make it easy to create this elegant appetizer. Creamy sweet polenta is paired with woodsy, earthy mushrooms for a medley of flavors and textures. You can brown the polenta slices in advance and warm the browned polenta in the microwave or under the broiler when you're ready to serve.

- -

1 (18-oz) tube pre-cooked Organic Polenta, cut into ½-inch slices
2 Tbsp olive oil, divided
¼ tsp black pepper
2 cups sliced crimini mushrooms
½ tsp salt
¼ cup Freshly Shredded Parmesan Cheese or Crumbled Goat Cheese
Chopped chives (optional)

1   Heat a large nonstick skillet or grill pan over high heat.
2   Drizzle 1 Tbsp olive oil onto hot pan. Arrange polenta slices in pan in a single layer. Sprinkle with black pepper. Cook for 4 minutes on each side, or until lightly browned.
3   While polenta is cooking, heat remaining 1 Tbsp olive oil in a small pan. Cook mushrooms for 5 minutes, sprinkling in salt toward the end. Remove from heat.
4   Top each polenta round with a heaping spoonful of mushrooms and a sprinkle of cheese. Garnish with chives.

Prep and cooking time: *20 minutes*
Serves *4*

Nutrition Snapshot
Per serving: 192 calories, 11 g fat, 3 g saturated fat, 7 g protein, 19 g carbs, 1 g fiber, 2 g sugar, 716 mg sodium

Vegetarian

Instant Homemade Guacamole

Stir salsa into ripe, mashed avocado to create instant guacamole without the effort of chopping and mixing multiple ingredients. Adjust heat by varying the amount and spiciness of the salsa you use. Trista Dedmon from Austin, Texas, recommends stirring in garlic and a fresh salsa such as Pico de Gallo. Serve guacamole with tortilla chips, veggie sticks, or your favorite Mexican dish.

. . . .

> 2 ripe avocados
> Juice of ½ lime
> 2 Tbsp Chunky Salsa, refrigerated Pico de Gallo, or other salsa
> I tsp finely chopped cilantro or parsley, or 1 cube frozen Chopped Cilantro (optional)

1 In a small bowl, mash avocado. Stir in lime juice.
2 Add salsa and cilantro, stirring just until combined. Do not overmix, or guacamole will turn grayish from salsa blending into avocados.

Prep time: *5 minutes*
Serves *4*

Nutrition Snapshot
Per serving: 118 calories, 11 g fat, 1 g saturated fat, 1 g protein, 7 g carbs, 5 g fiber, 1 g sugar, 65 mg sodium

Macho Nacho

Our Macho Nacho is a casserole version of a nachos plate, with lots of crunch and flavor. It's a substantial dish with chili and fresh toppings, making it a nice quick dinner or an easy appetizer. Don't forget this recipe on game day!

. . . .

8 oz corn tortilla chips (we used ½ of a 16-oz bag Organic White Corn Tortilla Chips)

1 (15-oz) can of your favorite chili (we like Organic Vegetarian Chili)

1 ½ cups Fancy Shredded Mexican Blend cheese

2 cups chopped tomato or quartered cherry tomatoes

1 cup (one tray) refrigerated Avocado's Number Guacamole

½ cup sour cream

½ cup Double Roasted Salsa or Chunky Salsa

¼ cup chopped fresh cilantro

1　Preheat oven to 375° F.

2　Scatter tortilla chips in a 9 x 13-inch baking pan and top with chili and cheese. Place pan in the oven for 10 minutes or until cheese is melted.

3　Take pan out of the oven and immediately add tomatoes, guacamole, and sour cream. Drizzle salsa over the top and sprinkle with cilantro. Serve immediately.

Prep and cooking time: *15-20 minutes*
Serves 8

Nutrition Snapshot
Per serving: 357 calories, 22 g fat, 6 g saturated fat, 10 g protein, 30 g carbs, 6 g fiber, 3 g sugar, 550 mg sodium

Chicken Satay with Peanut Sauce

A friend once joked that all food tastes better on a stick. He may have been on to something. Grilled chicken is healthy but can get boring. Thread it on skewers and *voilà*! Instant personality! The trick to juicy grilled chicken is to marinate the meat and grill at high temperature for just a few minutes. (If you don't want to heat the grill or broiler, pan-fry the chicken.) Don't overcook the meat or it will dry out. Leftovers can be de-skewered, cut into pieces and substituted for cooked chicken in any of our recipes.

. . . .

Chicken Satay

1 lb chicken tenders, or chicken breast cut into strips

½ cup light coconut milk

2 Tbsp peanut butter

1 tsp curry powder

2 cloves garlic, crushed, or 2 cubes frozen Crushed Garlic

2 tsp tamari or wheat-free soy sauce

Wooden skewers, soaked in water for 15 minutes or more

Peanut Sauce

½ cup light coconut milk

1 Tbsp peanut butter

2 tsp brown sugar

1 tsp tamari or wheat-free soy sauce

½ tsp curry powder

1 Combine coconut milk, peanut butter, curry, garlic, and tamari in large glass bowl. Add chicken and toss to coat. Cover and refrigerate for at least 30 minutes and up to overnight.

2 To prepare peanut sauce, place all ingredients in a small saucepan over medium-low heat. Simmer for 5 minutes, stirring frequently. Remove from heat and cool before serving. Sauce will thicken as it cools.

3 When ready to cook chicken, preheat grill or broiler. Thread chicken strips onto skewers.

4 Grill for 2-3 minutes per side, or until done. Cooking time will vary depending on thickness of chicken.

Prep and cooking time: *20 minutes (not counting marinating time)*
Makes *8 skewers*

Nutrition Snapshot
Per skewer with 1½ tsp sauce: 168 calories, 8 g fat, 4 g saturated fat, 19 g protein, 4 g carbs, 1 g fiber, 1 g sugar, 348 mg sodium

Eggplant Tostada

This dish is similar to a Mexican tostada, a flat tortilla that is toasted. The eggplant spread acts as a glue to keep toppings from falling off. Get creative with this dish and top it with any ingredients you have on hand, including seafood, chicken, or leftover vegetables.

. . . .

4 brown rice tortillas or other gluten-free tortillas

1 cup Eggplant Garlic Spread or Red Pepper Spread with Eggplant & Garlic

1 cup tomatoes, chopped

½ cup Crumbled Feta cheese

2 Tbsp chopped parsley

1 Preheat oven to 400° F.

2 Cover each tortilla with ¼ cup eggplant spread and place on baking sheet. Top with tomatoes and feta.

3 Bake for 10-12 minutes or until tortillas are golden and crisp on the edges.

4 Garnish with a sprinkle of parsley.

Variation: *For a Mexican version, use Refried Black Bean Dip and top with tomatoes, corn, shredded cheddar cheese, and cilantro.*

Prep time: *5 minutes*
Hands-off cooking time: *10- 12 minutes*
Serves *4*

Nutrition Snapshot
Per serving: 318 calories, 15 g fat, 3 g saturated fat, 6 g protein, 35 g carbs, 4 g fiber, 11 g sugar, 963 mg sodium

Cinnamon-Pear Baked Brie

Baked Brie is one of the world's easiest and tastiest appetizers. Trader Joe's has a wide selection of soft and creamy Brie cheeses. During the holidays, they also have small Brie wheels in addition to their usual wedges. This recipe comes from Stephanie King in Petaluma, California, who noted that the lightness of the pear chunks is a terrific contrast to the richness of Brie. Try substituting fresh Asian pears when they are in season.

. . . .

1 (8 or 12-oz) Brie wheel or 1 large wedge Brie
½ (25-oz) jar Pear Halves in White Grape Juice, or 2 fresh pears, peeled and cored
Scant ¼ tsp cinnamon
2 Tbsp chopped pecans or hazelnuts (optional)

1 Preheat oven to 350˚ F.
2 Slice off the very top rind of the Brie and discard. Place Brie inside a small oven-proof dish, cut face up.
3 Cut 3-4 pear halves into big chunks and scatter over top of Brie.
4 Sprinkle cinnamon and nuts over pears.
5 Bake for 20-30 minutes, or until Brie is softened and starting to melt (but before it gets runny).
6 Serve with toasted gluten-free bread or rice crackers.

Prep time: *5 minutes*
Hands-off cooking time: *20-30 minutes*
Serves *8*

Nutrition Snapshot
Per serving (not including nuts): 116 calories, 8 g fat, 5 g saturated fat, 6 g protein, 6 g carbs, 1 g fiber, 4 g sugar, 178 mg sodium

Spicy Tropical Shrimp Boats

All aboard! Shrimp, mango, and jalapeños set sail on endive boats. No utensils needed for this seafood adventure. The sweet flavors in the fruit salsa offset the slightly bitter taste of crunchy endive. Be prepared for the salsa's spicy kick!

· ·

1 cup frozen Medium Cooked Tail-Off Shrimp, thawed
½ cup Fire Roasted Papaya Mango Salsa
Salt and pepper
1 head fresh Belgian endive, leaves separated
2 Tbsp refrigerated Cilantro Dressing
Cilantro for garnish

1 Dice shrimp into cubes. Mix shrimp and salsa. Season with salt and pepper to taste.
2 Spoon shrimp mixture onto endive leaves. Arrange shrimp boats on serving platter and drizzle with dressing.
3 Garnish with cilantro.

Variation: *For a more traditional (and less spicy) shrimp salad, omit salsa and instead mix ¼ cup Cilantro Dressing or other creamy dressing into the shrimp. Garnish with cilantro.*

Prep time: *15 minutes*
Serves *4 (2 boats each)*

Nutrition Snapshot
Per serving: 101 calories, 3 g fat, 0 g saturated fat, 14 g protein, 5 g carbs, 0 g fiber, 3 g sugar, 524 mg sodium

Wasabi Eggs

Deviled eggs get sassy with a kick of wasabi! Kate Smith from Walnut Creek, California, sent us this recipe and says whenever she takes this dish to a potluck, she never has leftovers to take home. For another flavor variation, she suggests trying ½ tsp curry powder along with regular mayonnaise. Boil your own eggs (see our Helpful Tip below) or buy Trader Joe's ready-to-eat hard boiled and peeled eggs.

. . . .

1 dozen hard-boiled eggs

⅓ cup reduced-fat or regular mayonnaise

1½ Tbsp Wasabi Mayonnaise (more if you prefer more heat)

½ tsp 21 Seasoning Salute

2 Tbsp pickle relish (optional)

Paprika (optional)

1 Peel eggs, slice in half lengthwise, and empty yolks into a bowl.
2 Mash yolks with a fork and add remaining ingredients except paprika. Mix well.
3 Spoon egg yolk filling into egg white halves. Sprinkle lightly with paprika.

Prep time: *15 minutes*
Serves *12 (2 pieces per serving)*

Nutrition Snapshot
Per serving (not including relish): 112 calories, 9 g fat, 2 g saturated fat, 6 g protein, 1 g carbs, 0 g fiber, 1 g sugar, 125 mg sodium

> **Helpful Tip:**
> *A ring of green around the yolk occurs when an egg cooks for too long or at too high a temperature. Use this fail-safe method to avoid the green ring. Place eggs in a pot and fill with water to cover by 1 inch. Place over medium-high flame and heat to boiling. Boil for 1 minute, then remove from heat and let rest, covered, for 10 minutes.*

Vegetarian

Bacon Wrapped Dates

You don't have to choose between salty and sweet. You can have both in this indulgent combination of crisp bacon and sweet chewy dates. Medjool dates are quite large, so we use half for each appetizer bite. With smaller dates, use them whole.

1 lb bacon, sliced in half
½ lb (half pkg) Medjool dates, about 12
24 toothpicks or small bamboo skewers

1 Preheat oven to 400° F.
2 Remove pits from dates and slice in half lengthwise. Wrap each date half with bacon slice, using a toothpick to secure the end.
3 Place on a broiling rack, which allows grease to drip as bacon is cooking. Bake for 25-30 minutes, flipping halfway during baking.

Prep time: *15 minutes*
Hands-off cooking time: *25-30 minutes*
Serves *12 (2 pieces per serving)*

Nutrition Snapshot
Per serving: 169 calories, 7 g fat, 2 g saturated fat, 6 g protein, 23 g carbs, 2 g fiber, 20 g sugar, 378 mg sodium

Did you know?
Studies have shown that ounce for ounce, dates have the highest anti-oxidant levels of any fruit!

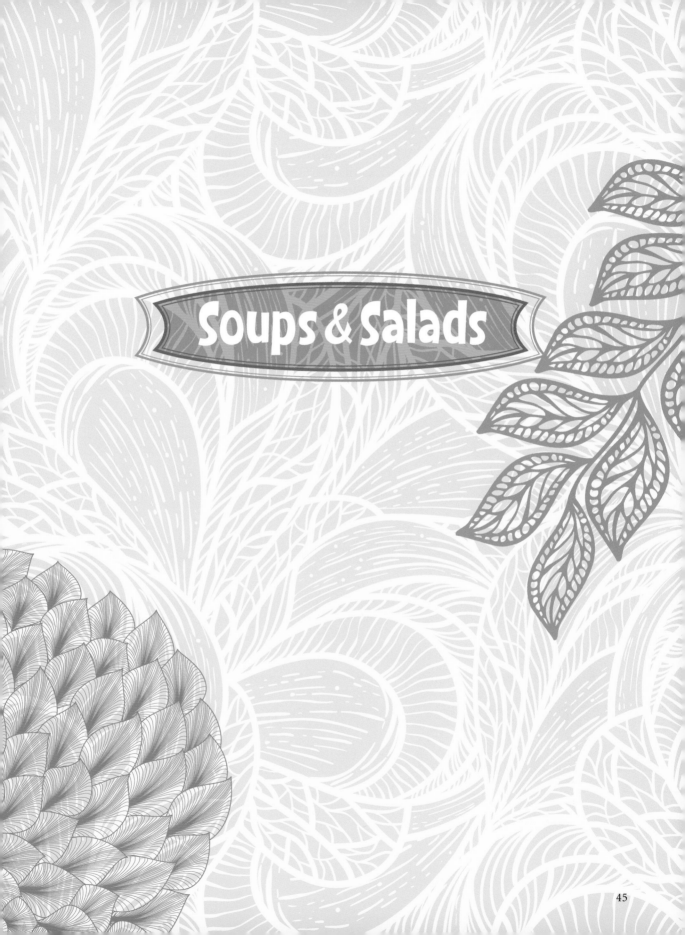

Soups & Salads

Cool as Cucumber Soup

A chilled soup - especially one fragrant with fresh cucumber and mint - hits the spot on a summer day. This soup requires nothing but a blender, so you won't spend even a minute over a hot stove. Serve with gluten-free crackers or toasted gluten-free bread.

. . . .

1 lb Persian cucumbers (or other thin-skinned cucumber), unpeeled
1 cup plain yogurt such as Plain Cream Line Yogurt
¼ cup packed fresh mint leaves
½ tsp salt
2 tsp seasoned rice vinegar
Black pepper

1 Chop cucumbers into 1-inch pieces.
2 Add all ingredients to blender and purée until smooth.
3 Serve sprinkled with pepper. Garnish with extra yogurt and mint leaves, if desired.

Prep time: *5 minutes*
Makes *4 (¾-cup) servings*

Nutrition Snapshot
Per serving: 57 calories, 1 g fat, 1 g saturated fat, 4 g protein, 9 g carbs, 1 g fiber, 6 g sugar, 336 mg sodium

Vegetarian

Chicken Tortilla Soup

This warm, flavorful soup is sure to cure the common cold and the common soup. The best part is the contrast of fresh cilantro, fresh avocado, cheese, and crispy chips added at the last minute to this aromatic, spicy soup. It's *delicioso* - make extra!

- -

4 boneless chicken thighs

3 cups gluten-free chicken broth

2 cups water

1 yellow onion, quartered

1 tsp ground cumin

¾ cup Chunky Salsa

2 Tbsp lime juice (juice of 1 lime)

¼ cup chopped fresh cilantro

Toppings for each bowl

Handful of broken tortilla chips or strips

¼ cup Fancy Shredded Mexican Blend cheese

¼ of a ripe avocado, diced

1   Combine water, broth, and onion in a pot and bring to a boil. Add chicken, salsa, and cumin; boil until the chicken is poached, about 10 minutes.

2   Remove large onion pieces and discard. Using two forks, coarsely shred chicken and return to pot.

3   Add lime and simmer for an additional 5 minutes.

4   Remove pot from heat and add cilantro.

5   Ladle soup into individual bowls. Add broken tortilla chips, cheese, and avocado chunks to each bowl. Serve immediately.

Prep and cooking time: *20 minutes*
Serves *4*

Nutrition Snapshot
Per serving: 383 calories, 25 g fat, 9 g saturated fat, 22 g protein, 20 g carbs, 5 g fiber, 7 g sugar, 977 mg sodium

Mulligatawny

The first time most of us heard of mulligatawny was on Seinfeld's "Soup Nazi" episode, as Kramer's favorite soup. No wonder people were willing to wait in line for this fantastic soup of vegetables, sweet apples, mild curry, and creamy yogurt. We make a lightning-fast version using prepared mirepoix, a ready-made curry sauce, and all-natural applesauce. The soup is mild enough that kids will love eating it as much as they'll love saying the name.

. . . .

1 (14.5-oz) container Mirepoix, or 1 cup each chopped onions, celery, and carrots

1 Tbsp olive oil

1 boneless chicken breast, diced

1 cup unsweetened applesauce

1 (15-oz) jar Masala Simmer Sauce

1 (14.5-oz) can diced tomatoes with no salt added

½ cup plain yogurt such as Plain Cream Line Yogurt

1 pouch frozen Organic Jasmine Rice, or 2 cups cooked rice

1 In a medium pot over high heat, add oil and sauté mirepoix for 4 minutes. Add chicken and brown for an additional minute.

2 Add applesauce, Masala Simmer Sauce, and tomato. Bring to a boil and simmer for 5 minutes. Meanwhile prepare frozen rice according to package instructions (3 minutes in microwave).

3 Take out ½ cup of soup and slowly stir into yogurt (this will temper the yogurt) and then add mixture back into soup, stirring well. This soup is meant to be thick, but if you'd like it thinner, add water or broth.

4 Place a scoop of rice in each bowl, add soup, and top with a little more rice.

Prep and cooking time: *15 minutes*
Makes *8 (1 cup plus ¼ cup rice) servings*

Nutrition Snapshot
Per serving: 197 calories, 7 g fat, 2 g saturated fat, 10 g protein,
25 g carbs, 3 g fiber, 14 g sugar, 247 mg sodium

Vegetarian

Omit chicken. Stir in 1-2 cups cooked quinoa, if desired, for extra protein.

Helpful Tip:
When adding yogurt to a very hot soup or curry, temper the yogurt by adding some soup to warm up the yogurt. If you add cold yogurt directly to a hot soup, the yogurt may curdle.

Watermelon Cucumber Salad

Crisp, juicy, and ultra refreshing, watermelon cucumber salad embodies summer in a bowl. It's a welcome side dish to any barbecue. We use Persian cucumbers, which are small, seedless, and thin-skinned, so you don't need to peel them. Yellow cherry tomatoes add happy sunny color. Experiment with other additions such as crunchy jicama, sweet orange segments, or a sprinkle of feta cheese.

. . . .

3 cups cubed watermelon

3 cups cubed Persian cucumber (peel and seed if using regular cucumbers)

2 cups chopped tomatoes (optional)

3 Tbsp fresh lime juice (juice from 1-1½ limes)

Pinch salt

¼ cup chopped fresh basil, cilantro, or mint

1 Place watermelon, cucumber, and tomatoes in a large bowl. Add lime juice and salt, and toss gently to coat. Garnish with basil.

2 Let sit for 15 minutes before serving. If making ahead, store in fridge.

Prep time: *15 minutes*
Serves *8*

Nutrition Snapshot
Per serving: 26 calories, 0 g fat, 0 g saturated fat, 1 g protein, 6 g carbs, 1 g fiber, 4 g sugar, 14 mg sodium

Black Bean and Ricotta-Stuffed Portabellas

Everyone who first sees this recipe thinks, "Black beans and ricotta - are you sure?" but follow up with, "Wow, it really works!" We wouldn't steer you wrong. The fillings have lots of complementary flavors and textures, and the Portabellas are a hearty and substantial base. This tasty recipe can really do triple duty as an appetizer, side dish, or light dinner.

2 large Portabella mushroom caps
½ cup ricotta cheese
½ cup canned black beans
2 Tbsp refrigerated Fresh Bruschetta Sauce
½ cup shredded mozzarella cheese

1 Preheat oven to 400° F.
2 Don't wash the Portabellas. Instead use a mushroom brush or a clean kitchen towel to wipe the caps.
3 Cut stems completely off the Portabella caps, and place caps upside down on an oiled baking sheet or pan. Combine ricotta and black beans. Spread this mixture inside the caps. Do not overfill since caps will shrink slightly as they cook. Add 1 Tbsp bruschetta sauce on top of the filling and top each cap with mozzarella.
4 Bake for 12-14 minutes. Do not overcook or the Portabellas will cook down and get very watery. Serve immediately.

Prep time: *5 minutes*
Hands-off cooking time: *12-14 minutes*
Serves *2*

Nutrition Snapshot
Per serving: 341 calories, 16 g fat, 11 g saturated fat, 27 g protein, 18 g carbs, 5 g fiber, 3 g sugar, 434 mg sodium

Warm Spinach Salad

This salad combines the smokiness of bacon with the richness of avocado, the earthiness of mushrooms, and the tang of balsamic vinaigrette. Fresh baby spinach hosts the party of ingredients. Fully cooked bacon, available at Trader Joe's, avoids the messy splatter of cooking bacon. In similar salads, the dressing is often made with the leftover bacon grease, but we use heart-healthy extra virgin olive oil instead.

1 (6-oz) bag baby spinach

4 strips bacon (Fully Cooked Uncured Bacon or uncooked bacon)

1 (8-oz) container white mushrooms, sliced, or 1 (10-oz) bag Sliced White Mushrooms

1 ripe avocado, diced or sliced

For balsamic vinaigrette (or use ⅓ cup of your favorite vinaigrette)

4 Tbsp extra virgin olive oil

2 Tbsp balsamic vinegar

1 tsp honey or agave nectar

1 Crisp fully-cooked bacon in pan and remove. If using uncooked bacon, cook in pan and remove bacon. Drain excess grease.

2 In the same pan, sauté mushrooms for 3-4 minutes, until mushrooms are plump and before they begin to release water. Do not overcook.

3 Whisk together vinaigrette ingredients and toss with spinach. Add warm mushrooms.

4 Crumble bacon on top, add avocado, and toss gently.

Prep and cooking time: *15 minutes*
Serves *4*

Nutrition Snapshot
Per serving: 256 calories, 22 g fat, 4 g saturated fat,
6 g protein, 10 g carbs, 5 g fiber, 4 g sugar, 217 mg sodium

Substitute vegetarian bacon

> **Helpful Tip:**
> *Let avocados ripen on the counter. Never place avocados in fridge unless they are fully ripe, because the cold prevents them from ripening. When an avocado yields gently to the touch, it's ready. To dice an avocado, start by cutting it in half and removing the pit. With a sharp knife, make crosshatched cuts. Spoon the cubes of avocado out of the skin.*

Posh Mâche Salad

Mâche (pronounced "mosh"), also known as lamb's lettuce, is a delicate, buttery-textured lettuce with small rounded leaves. Toss with a mild dressing, such as our lemon vinaigrette below, to enjoy its subtle flavors. To complete this salad, we add fresh fruits and Trader Joe's addictive sesame honey coated cashews.

1 (4-oz) bag mâche
2 kiwi, peeled and sliced
1 cup sliced strawberries
½ cup Sesame Honey Cashews

For lemon vinaigrette

3 Tbsp extra virgin olive oil
1 Tbsp lemon juice
1 tsp honey
Pinch salt and black pepper

1 In a salad bowl, combine mache, kiwi, strawberries, and cashews.
2 Whisk the dressing ingredients until emulsified and pour over salad, giving a toss to coat.

Prep time: *10 minutes*
Serves *4*

Nutrition Snapshot
Per serving: 213 calories, 16 g fat, 2 g saturated fat, 3 g protein, 16 g carbs, 11 g sugar, 2 g fiber, 48 mg sodium

Potato and Kale Soup

This quintessential winter soup stars kale, a leafy winter vegetable. Grab fresh kale when it's in season - it's packed with nutrition and antioxidants. This recipe has a Latin spin, similar to Caldo Verde, a popular Portuguese soup. By cooking kale (or spinach) for just a few minutes, the leaves retain their vibrant green color. The bright blended greens make a pesto–like base for the soup, with larger chunks of kale and potato lending a satisfying heartiness. Sausage or chorizo chunks can be added for an extra punch of flavor and protein. Substitute spinach or Trader Joe's Southern Greens blend if kale is not available.

- -

1 Tbsp olive oil

1 large onion, chopped, or 2 cups refrigerated Diced Onions

2 cloves garlic, crushed, or 2 cubes frozen Crushed Garlic

6 cups gluten-free chicken or vegetable broth

1 lb potatoes, diced into ½-inch cubes

1 large bunch kale, chopped, or 1 (6-oz) bag baby spinach

Salt and black pepper

2 smoked sausage or chorizo links, cooked and chopped (optional)

1   Heat olive oil in a large pot. Add onion and sauté until soft, about 5 minutes. Add garlic and cook 1-2 minutes longer.
2   Pour in broth, potatoes, and chopped kale stems (these cook longer than the leaves). Bring mixture to boil. Cover, lower heat, and simmer for 10 minutes until potatoes are almost tender.
3   Increase heat and add remaining kale (or spinach). Cook for 5 minutes until leaves turn bright green. Do not overcook.
4   Blend half of the soup using an immersion blender or regular blender. Return soup to pot and check for seasonings, adding salt and pepper to taste. Top with sausage.

Prep and cooking time: *20 minutes*
Hands-off cooking time: *15 minutes*
Serves *8*

Nutrition Snapshot
Per serving (not including sausage): 112 calories, 2 g fat, 0 g saturated fat, 5 g protein, 20 g carbs, 4 g fiber, 298 mg sodium

Use vegetable broth or water. Omit sausage or use vegetarian sausage.

Taco Soup

Taco soup combines the flavors and textures we all love about tacos into a hearty soup. One-pot meals like this are great for crowds because each person can tailor the toppings according to their own tastes, and you can serve it all buffet style. A soup is also easier to handle than tacos, especially for young kids. Offer guests any combination of toppings (suggestions listed below recipe). Tortilla chips are mandatory.

. . . .

1.5 lbs boneless chicken breasts or thighs

1 Tbsp olive oil

1 medium onion, chopped, or 1½ cups refrigerated Diced Onions

1 (1.3-oz) pkg Taco Seasoning Mix (for milder palates, use half the package)

1 (28-oz) can diced tomatoes, undrained

2 (15-oz) cans black beans, drained

1 (15-oz) can corn, drained, or 1½ cups frozen corn

2 cups gluten-free chicken broth

Your choice of toppings - suggestions include:

Tortilla chips	Shredded cheese	Chopped green onions or red onions
Fresh cilantro	Avocado	
Sour cream	Chopped tomatoes	Jalapeños or chiles

1   In a large pot, heat olive oil over medium-high heat. Sauté onion until soft, about 5 minutes.
2   Add remaining ingredients and heat to boiling. Cover, reduce heat to low, and simmer for 1 hour.
3   Remove chicken, shred, and return to pot. Stir and heat through.
4   Serve with your choice of toppings.

Variation: *Slow cooker method: Place all ingredients into a crockpot and cook for 5-6 hours on low setting. Remove chicken, shred, and return to crockpot. Stir and heat through before serving.*

Prep time: *15 minutes*
Hands-off cooking time: *1 hour*
Makes *8 (1-cup) servings*

Nutrition Snapshot
Per serving: 239 calories, 3 g fat, 0.5 g saturated fat, 13 g protein, 22 g carbs, 6 g fiber, 7 g sugar, 475 mg sodium

Vegetarian

Omit chicken and use vegetable broth or water

Homemade Blue Cheese Dressing

We skipped the mayonnaise and sour cream used in traditional blue cheese dressings and created one using Greek yogurt and buttermilk. The star component of this dressing is tangy blue cheese, complemented with lemon and garlic. Enjoy this dressing over sweet and light lettuces, such as iceberg, Romaine, or butter lettuce. The dressing will keep for several days in the refrigerator in a covered container or jar.

· ·

4 oz (½ container) Crumbled Salem Blue cheese

½ cup cultured low-fat (1%) buttermilk

½ cup non-fat Greek yogurt

1 Tbsp lemon juice

1 clove garlic, crushed, or 1 cube frozen Crushed Garlic, thawed

Black pepper

Dried cranberries for garnish (optional)

1 Combine buttermilk, yogurt, lemon, and garlic. Gently stir in blue cheese and season to taste with pepper.

2 Serve dressing over butter lettuce or wedges of iceberg lettuce and garnish with cranberries.

Variation: *If using plain yogurt instead of thick Greek yogurt, use 1 cup plain yogurt and omit buttermilk or the dressing will be too runny.*

Prep time: *5 minutes*

Makes *10 (2-Tbsp) servings*

Nutrition Snapshot
Per serving (not including garnish): 52 calories, 3 g fat, 2 g saturated fat, 4 g protein, 2 g carbs, 0 g fiber, 1 g sugar, 173 mg sodium

Mediterranean Lentil Salad

Tender pre-cooked lentils make this salad a mix-and-serve breeze. The light, lemony, fresh taste makes it a great side dish or light lunch. It's a terrific potluck or party item because you can make it ahead and serve at room temperature. Use leftovers in a wrap with hummus, roasted veggies, or Greek yogurt.

• •

1 (17.6-oz) pkg refrigerated Steamed Lentils (about 2 ½ cups)
1 ½ cups chopped tomato (we like to use cocktail tomatoes or baby Romas in this recipe)
½ cup chopped fresh parsley
1 Tbsp fresh mint (optional)
1 Tbsp lemon juice
2 Tbsp extra virgin olive oill

1 Combine lentils, tomatoes, parsley, and mint.
2 Whisk together lemon juice and olive oil. Pour dressing over salad, stirring gently to combine.

Prep time: *5 minutes,* **Serves** *6*

Nutrition Snapshot
Per serving: 227 calories, 7 g fat, 1 g saturated fat, 14 g protein, 29 g carbs, 11 g fiber, 4 g sugar, 308 mg sodium

Pesto Gazpacho

Our twist on the traditional gazpacho pays homage to the Italian flavors of pine nuts and fresh basil. We like the flavor of raw pine nuts in this recipe, but if the taste is too "piney" for you, toast the nuts. This soup is great at room temperature!

- -

4 cups (one 32-oz carton) Organic Creamy Tomato Soup
2 Tbsp fresh basil
½ cup raw pine nuts

1 Combine all ingredients in a blender, saving a bit of basil and pine nuts for garnish.
2 Pureé until smooth. Serve topped with basil and pine nuts.

Prep time: *10 minutes*
Serves *4*

Nutrition Snapshot
Per serving:
205 calories, 12 g fat,
2 g saturated fat,
8 g protein, 17 g carbs,
2 g fiber, 11 g sugar,
750 mg sodium

Warm Goat Cheese Salad

Goat cheese rounds are heated just enough to create a crusty layer without melting the cheese. This restaurant favorite is easy to make at home, especially with pre-sliced goat cheese medallions. We use almond meal instead of traditional breadcrumbs, both for flavor and nutritional value.

. . . .

1 (5.4-oz) pkg Chevre Medallions or 1 (8-oz) log Chevre goat cheese, sliced

1 egg white, beaten

½ cup almond meal or ground almonds

2 Tbsp olive oil

1 (5-oz) bag Organics Baby Spring Mix salad

⅓ cup refrigerated Champagne Pear Vinaigrette or your favorite dressing

1   Dip each goat cheese round in egg white and then coat in almond meal. If you're prepping ahead of time, place breaded goat cheese rounds in refrigerator until ready to cook. Cheese rounds should be cold and firm so they don't melt when fried.

2   Heat olive oil in a nonstick pan over medium heat. Fry cheese rounds for 1 minute on each side or until browned. Promptly remove from heat before cheese melts.

3   Pour vinaigrette over salad mix and toss until coated. Place warm cheese on dressed salad and serve immediately.

Prep and cooking time: *20 minutes*
Serves *4*

Nutrition Snapshot
Per serving: 392 calories, 29 g fat, 15 g saturated fat, 20 g protein, 13 g carbs, 1 g fiber, 5 g sugar, 376 mg sodium

Tip: *If you're slicing a goat cheese log yourself, don't use a knife or you'll end up with a gooey mess. Using unflavored dental floss, hold both ends tightly and press taut floss down through goat cheese.*

Vegetarian

Breakout Broccoli Salad

Boring broccoli salad takes on a new life with zesty dressing, crunchy rosemary-infused almonds, and tart cherries. Instead of steaming the broccoli, we blanch it briefly, bringing out the vibrant green color and retaining all the crunch. To cut down the prep time, skip the blanching and use raw broccoli. You can also substitute your favorite ready-made creamy dressing for the homemade one here.

1 (12-oz) bag Organic Broccoli Florets, or 6 cups of broccoli cut into bite-size pieces
¼ cup dried Tart Montmorency Cherries or raisins
⅓ cup Marcona Almonds with Rosemary, roughly chopped or sliced almonds
Pinch salt

For dressing

3 Tbsp mayonnaise

1 tsp red wine vinegar

1 tsp lemon juice

1 tsp sugar

1   Bring 6 cups of water to boil. Add broccoli to boiling water, wait 10 seconds, and then drain. Rinse with cold water and leave to drain and cool.
2   Whisk together dressing ingredients and toss broccoli with dressing. Add cherries, almonds, and salt, tossing again.

Prep and cooking time: *10 minutes*
Serves *4*

Nutrition Snapshot
Per serving: 224 calories, 15 g fat, 2 g saturated fat, 6 g protein, 21 g carbs, 5 g fiber, 10 g sugar, 177 mg sodium

Spicy Shrimp Soup

Mary Marlowe Leverette from Columbia, South Carolina, sent us this wonderful recipe, which combines the complexity of curry and the tang of buttermilk. It's an exotic combination of flavors. Mary normally serves this soup cold, but we liked it equally well warm.

- -

1 ½ lbs small, shelled shrimp

3 Tbsp olive oil

1 small sweet onion, finely diced

1 Tbsp mild curry powder

2 cloves garlic, crushed, or 2 cubes frozen Crushed Garlic

1 (16-oz) bag frozen white corn kernels, thawed

3 cups buttermilk

¼ tsp sea salt

1 tsp freshly ground black pepper

1-2 tsp Tabasco or other hot pepper sauce

2 Tbsp freshly minced chives

1   Heat oil over medium heat and sauté onion, curry and garlic until onion is translucent. Add shrimp and sauté until shrimp is just pink - about five minutes. Remove from heat and cool completely.

2   Place 2 cups corn and the buttermilk in food processor and blend until smooth. Transfer to large storage container.

3   Add remaining corn, shrimp mixture, salt and Tabasco, stirring well. Cover and refrigerate for at least 2 hours. Serve soup in chilled bowls, sprinkling top with chives.

Prep and cooking time: *10 minutes*
Serves *4*

Nutrition Snapshot
Per serving: 464 calories, 16 g fat, 3 g saturated fat, 45 g protein, 39 g carbs, 3 g fiber, 10 g sugar, 628 mg sodium

Life is a Bowl of Cherries, Pine Nuts, and Spinach Salad

The creation of this salad was a complete accident. Deana was at a potluck pottery workshop where she tried a tasty salad and asked the person who made it for the recipe. When she met the woman again, she thanked her for the recipe and told her that the pine nuts, cherries, and feta were amazing with the spinach. She laughed and said her salad recipe was arugula with blue cheese, walnuts, and apples. So much for memory... we still need to try her version. Montmorency cherries are the most popular sour cherry in the U.S., and they give a great sweet yet tart balance to the feta and pine nuts in this spinach salad. This salad is high in antioxidants from the cherries and in folic acid from the spinach (highest when raw).

1 (6-oz) bag baby spinach

½ cup Crumbled Feta cheese

½ cup dried Tart Montmorency Cherries

½ cup toasted pine nuts

6 Tbsp Balsamic Vinaigrette, or make your own (recipe below)

1 Combine ingredients, toss, and serve immediately.

2 The salad can be assembled ahead of time, but don't add the vinaigrette until you're ready to serve, or the spinach will wilt down.

Prep time: *5 minutes*
Serves *4*

Homemade Balsamic Vinaigrette

4 Tbsp extra virgin olive oil

2 Tbsp balsamic vinegar

¼ tsp dried basil

¼ tsp Dijon mustard

¼ tsp honey or a pinch of sugar

1 Whisk together vinaigrette ingredients.

2 Vinaigrette keeps for a few days in a closed container, such as a glass jar with a lid.

Nutrition Snapshot
Per serving: 249 calories, 22 g fat, 4 g saturated fat, 3 g protein, 14 g carbs, 2 g fiber, 9 g sugar, 151 mg sodium

Zesty Potato Salad

Swap out heavy mayo-based dressings in traditional potato salads with this tangy and bright balsamic vinaigrette. Use your choice of baby potatoes or tri-color potatoes in red, gold, and purple to liven up ordinary potato salad. Fresh raw green beans are packed full of nutrients and add a nice crunchy balance to soft potatoes.

. . . .

1 (28-oz) bag Red, Gold, and Purple Potatoes (called "Potato Medley") or baby potatoes
2 cups green beans, cut into ½-inch pieces
½ cup chopped fresh basil

For Dijon-balsamic vinaigrette (or use ½ cup of your favorite vinaigrette)
¼ cup extra virgin olive oil
¼ cup balsamic vinegar
2 tsp Dijon or stoneground mustard
1 clove garlic, crushed, or 1 cube frozen Crushed Garlic

1   Boil potatoes in salted water until fork-tender, about 20 minutes. Drain and do not peel.
2   Cut potatoes into bite-size pieces.
3   Place warm potatoes into bowl and add raw green beans.
4   Whisk together vinaigrette ingredients. Pour over potatoes and toss until coated.
5   Add basil and give final toss to combine. Serve warm or chilled.

Prep time: *10 minutes*
Hands-off cooking time: *20 minutes*
Serves *6*

Nutrition Snapshot
Per serving: 207 calories, 9 g fat, 1 g saturated fat, 4 g protein, 29 g carbs, 4 g fiber, 4 g sugar, 33 mg sodium

Le French Lentil Soup

The best, most delicate lentils are French lentils, but they take longer to cook than other varieties. Thanks to Trader Joe's imported pre-cooked lentils, this earthy soup can be made in minutes instead of hours. This recipe has fooled guests who staunchly claimed to dislike lentils, so test it on your own lentil-phobe. Ham or sausage makes this a hearty meal, but you can leave out the meat out for a vegetarian version.

· ·

1 (17.6-oz) pkg refrigerated Steamed Lentils (about 2 ½ cups)

2 Tbsp olive oil

1 large onion, chopped, or 2 cups bagged Freshly Diced Onions

1 cup sliced carrots

1 tsp ground cumin

4 cups (one 32-oz carton) gluten-free chicken or vegetable broth

1 cup diced Applewood Smoked Cured Ham (optional)

1 Tbsp fresh lemon juice

Salt and pepper to taste

2 Tbsp chopped cilantro

Sour cream (optional)

1   Heat olive oil in a large saucepan over medium-high heat.

2   Cook onions and carrots for 10 minutes or until onions soften. Stir in cumin and salt; cook for 1 minute longer to toast cumin.

3   Add chicken broth, lentils, and ham. Bring to a boil for a minute to heat everything through.

4   Remove from heat and stir in lemon juice. Add salt and pepper to taste.

5   Garnish with sour cream and cilantro.

Prep and cooking time: *20 minutes*
Serves *6*

Nutrition Snapshot
Per serving: 204 calories, 7 g fat, 1 g saturated fat, 14 g protein, 22 g carbs, 7 g fiber, 4 g sugar, 554 mg sodium

Omit ham and use vegetable broth or water

Black Bean Soup

One of our favorites. This soup is hearty and spicy, thanks to the warm earthy flavor of cumin and the zing of fresh lime. We like it with tortilla chips on the side. It makes a great meal by itself, or it can be paired with one of our quesadilla recipes for a bigger meal. Black beans are not only high in fiber and folate, they also rival grapes and cranberries for their antioxidant properties. Sensitive to sulfites? Black beans contain the trace mineral molybdenum, which counteracts sulfites. So uncork that bottle of red later tonight.

. . . .

1 medium yellow onion, peeled and chopped, or 1 ½ cups bagged Freshly Diced Onions

1 clove garlic, crushed, or 1 cube frozen Crushed Garlic

2 Tbsp extra virgin olive oil

1 tsp ground cumin

2 (15-oz) cans black beans (do not drain)

1 cup (half a jar) Chunky Salsa

2 Tbsp lime juice (juice of 1 lime)

Plain yogurt, such as Plain Cream Line Yogurt, or sour cream (optional)

1 In a medium pot, sauté onions in olive oil until they are soft and translucent.

2 Sprinkle in cumin and garlic and sauté for a minute; pour in black beans (including juices), salsa, and lime. Stir to combine and bring to a simmer. Simmer covered for 20 minutes.

3 Ladle soup into individual bowls and top with a dollop of yogurt.

Prep time: *10 minutes*
Hands-off cooking time: *20 minutes*
Serves *5*

Nutrition Snapshot
Per serving: 234 calories, 6 g fat, 1 g saturated fat,
9 g protein, 35 g carbs, 9 g fiber, 7 g sugar, 879 mg sodium

Zesty Shrimp and Scallops on Greens

The subtle sweet and spicy tones of the Pineapple Salsa and the fresh flavor of cilantro are tasty additions to shrimp and scallops. You can serve this dish as an impressive small starter salad or increase the portions for a healthy entrée. If you haven't discovered Trader Joe's Cilantro Dressing yet, you may be about to meet your favorite dressing.

Salad

½ (5-oz) bag Organics Baby Spring Mix

2 Tbsp refrigerated Cilantro Dressing

12 spears of fresh asparagus, cut into thirds

2 Tbsp extra virgin olive oil, divided

Salt and pepper to taste

Seafood

1 cup (½ lb or ½ bag) frozen Medium or Large Cooked Tail-Off Shrimp, thawed

1 cup (½ lb or ½ bag) frozen small or medium scallops, thawed and pat dry

½ cup Pineapple Salsa

1 Tbsp chopped fresh cilantro

1 Preheat oven to 400° F, if using fresh asparagus.

2 If using fresh asparagus, toss and coat asparagus in 1 Tbsp olive oil, season with salt and pepper, and bake for 10-15 minutes, depending on size of stalks.

3 While asparagus is roasting, sauté scallops in 1 Tbsp olive oil for 3-5 minutes or until opaque, adding shrimp at the very end. If using raw shrimp, cook them with the scallops. Add salsa and sauté for additional minute.

4 Toss spring greens with dressing and divide it among serving plates. Top with asparagus and seafood mixture, and garnish generously with cilantro.

Prep and cooking time: *15-20 minutes*
Serves *2 as an entrée*

Nutrition Snapshot
Per serving: 382 calories, 18 g fat, 3 g saturated fat, 45 g protein, 10 g carbs, 1 g fiber, 5 g sugar, 653 mg sodium

Strawberry and Gorgonzola Herb Salad

This delightful spring salad bursts with the flavor of sweet strawberry and the bite of Gorgonzola cheese. If strawberries aren't in season, substitute any fruit of your choice. We love the contrasting tastes of salads that combine greens with fruits, nuts, and cheese. Experiment with your own combinations: spinach with cranberries, pine nuts, and goat cheese; arugula with pear, pecans, and blue cheese - the list goes on and on, and they all work with the sweet tang of a simple vinaigrette.

1 (5-oz) bag Herb Salad Mix (about 4 cups)

1 ½ cups fresh sliced strawberries

½ cup Crumbled Gorgonzola cheese

1 cup Mixed Candied Nuts (or use plain/candied walnuts or pecans)

¼ cup bottled Balsamic Vinaigrette (or make your own by mixing 2 parts extra virgin olive oil with 1 part Balsamic vinegar)

1 Combine all ingredients.

2 Toss with of vinaigrette just before serving.

Prep time: *5 minutes*
Serves *4*

Nutrition Snapshot
Per serving: 355 calories, 31 g fat, 2 g saturated fat, 11 g protein, 13 g carbs, 5 g fiber, 6 g sugar, 299 mg sodium

Vegetarian

Ginger Coconut Soup with Greens

This light soup gets it creamy base from coconut milk flavored with garlic and ginger. Healthy greens and tasty squash add color and nutrition. Trader Joe's Southern Greens are a washed and chopped blend of mustard, turnip, collard, and spinach, but you can use any combination of leafy greens in this soup. Deana's kids always ask for seconds.

. . . .

1 medium onion, thinly sliced
1 Tbsp olive or vegetable oil
4 cups (one 32-oz carton) gluten-free chicken or vegetable broth
1 (14-oz) can light coconut milk (2 cups)
5 loosely packed cups Southern Greens or any combination of cooking greens
1 (12 to 16-oz) bag cubed butternut squash, sweet potato, or Harvest Blend
1 clove garlic, crushed, or 1 cube frozen Crushed Garlic
1 Tbsp grated fresh ginger
Pinch salt

1 In a medium pot over high heat, sauté onion in oil until soft, about 5 minutes.
2 Being careful to avoid splattering, add broth, coconut milk, greens, squash, garlic, ginger, and salt. The greens will seem voluminous at first but cook down quickly.
3 Bring to boil, then cover, reduce heat, and simmer for 10 minutes, or until squash is tender.

Prep and cooking time: *20 minutes*
Makes *8 (1-cup) servings*

Nutrition Snapshot
Per serving: 113 calories, 6 g fat, 3 g saturated fat, 4 g protein, 14 g carbs, 2 g fiber, 5 g sugar, 78 mg sodium

Helpful Tip:
If you buy ginger root and don't use it all, peel it, place it in a freezer bag, and store in the freezer. Whenever you need ginger, take out the root and grate or cut as much as you need. Don't let the unused portion of the root thaw – put it right back into the freezer after use.

Vegetarian

Use vegetable broth or water

Beet and Endive Salad

Take advantage of Trader Joe's ready-to-eat steamed beets to create this elegant salad. Mild red and white endive leaves are topped with colorful beets, candied walnuts, and tangy goat cheese.

. . . .

2-3 heads of endive with leaves separated and cut in halves and thirds, some whole

4 refrigerated Steamed and Peeled Baby Beets (½ pkg), sliced

½ cup Candied Walnuts (or substitute plain walnuts)

4 Tbsp (2 oz) goat cheese, in small chunks, or use Crumbled Goat Cheese

¼ cup bottled Balsamic Vinaigrette or Red Wine & Olive Oil Vinaigrette

Freshly ground black pepper

1   Divide the endive leaves among 4 salad plates.
2   Top with the beet slices, walnuts, and goat cheese.
3   Drizzle with vinaigrette and season with black pepper to taste.

Prep time: *10 minutes*
Serves *4*

Nutrition Snapshot
Per serving: 203 calories, 14 g fat, 3 g saturated fat, 4 g protein, 14 g carbs, 3 g fiber, 11 g sugar, 62 mg sodium

Vegetarian

Garden Gazpacho

Gazpacho is a tomato-based, raw vegetable soup invented in Spain. Because it is served cold, it is most popular during hot summer months. There's only one rule about making gazpacho, and that is to keep the veggies chunky. You want a soup that's gloriously thick, not runny, with big flecks of vegetables throughout. This recipe was purposely kept mild, but you can add jalapeños or serve with a bottle of Tabasco on the side for a spicy kick. For nearly instant gazpacho, try our Pesto Gazpacho on page 67.

- -

4 cups tomato juice or vegetable juice

4 Roma tomatoes, or substitute 1 (14.5-oz) can diced tomatoes

1 large bell pepper, either green or red

1 large cucumber, or 2-3 small Persian cucumbers

Half a red onion

3 cloves garlic, crushed, or 3 cubes frozen Crushed Garlic

¼ cup red wine vinegar

⅓ cup chopped fresh basil, parsley, or cilantro

Salt and pepper to taste (start with 1 tsp salt and ½ tsp black pepper)

1 Cut vegetables into 1-inch chunks. Place vegetables into a food processor, using short pulses so that vegetables are chopped, not puréed into juice. It works best to chop and process each vegetable separately, since some vegetables purée faster than others.

2 Combine all chopped vegetables in a large bowl. Add tomato juice, garlic, vinegar, basil, salt, and pepper. Stir until soup is well combined.

3 Chill at least 4 hours and preferably overnight. The longer the soup sits, the better the flavors combine. Serve cold.

Prep time: *20 minutes*
Makes *8 (1-cup) servings*

Nutrition Snapshot
Per serving: 44 calories, 0 g fat, 0 g saturated fat, 2 g protein, 9 g carbs, 2 g fiber, 6 g sugar, 590 mg sodium

Vegetarian

Shrimp and Avocado Salad

Remember the shrimp salad you had growing up, swimming in mayo and piled onto avocado halves? Our modern version is lighter, tastier, and more sophisticated. We use Chilean langostino tails, which taste like lobster. They don't appear often, so when they do, stock up. Shrimp is also delicious in this light salad.

. . . .

1 (12-oz) bag frozen cooked Langostino Tails, thawed, or ¾ lb frozen cooked shrimp, thawed

1 large ripe avocado, cut into wedges or bite-size chunks

1 grapefruit, peeled and segmented

1 (5-oz) bag butter lettuce

¼ cup chopped pistachios

For white wine vinaigrette (or use ⅓ cup of your favorite light-flavored vinaigrette)

2 Tbsp white wine vinegar

3 Tbsp olive oil

½ clove garlic, crushed, or ½ cube frozen Crushed Garlic

¼ tsp salt

1 Arrange butter lettuce onto serving platter or individual plates.
2 Lightly toss avocado and grapefruit pieces; acid from the grapefruit will keep avocado from turning brown. Place evenly on top of lettuce.
3 Toss langostino tails with vinaigrette. Scatter evenly on salad, drizzling any remaining vinaigrette on top.
4 Sprinkle with pistachios.

Prep time: *15 minutes*
Serves: *4*

Nutrition Snapshot
Per serving: 310 calories, 20 g fat, 3 g saturated fat, 20 g protein, 13 g carbs, 4 g fiber, 5 g sugar, 275 mg sodium

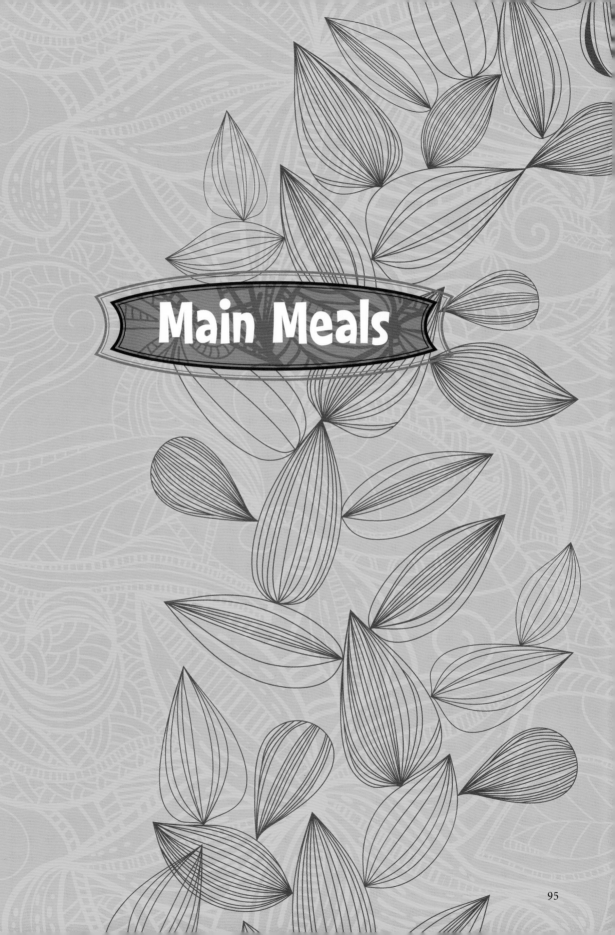

Main Meals

Shrimp Lettuce Wraps

Capture the flavor of restaurant lettuce wraps at home in minutes. Diced shrimp and veggies combined with the zing of an Asian-inspired sauce are wrapped in fresh iceberg lettuce leaves. This dish is best served family style, with the shrimp mixture in one bowl next to the lettuce leaves and optional toppings.

. . . .

1 lb large uncooked shrimp (peeled with tail off), thawed if frozen

2 Tbsp tamari or wheat-free soy sauce

1 tsp toasted sesame oil

1 clove garlic, crushed, or 1 cube frozen Crushed Garlic

1 Tbsp lemon or lime juice

2 green onions, chopped

1 Tbsp vegetable or olive oil

1 red bell pepper, diced, or 1 cup Mélange à Trois bell pepper strips, thawed

½ cup Shredded Carrots

5 shiitake mushrooms, thinly sliced

¼ tsp each salt and black pepper

1 head iceberg lettuce, leaves separated

Optional toppings

⅓ cup peanuts or Thai Lime Chile Cashews, roughly chopped

⅓ cup fresh basil, chopped

1 In a small bowl, combine tamari, sesame oil, garlic, lemon juice, and green onions to create a sauce. Set aside.

2 Dice shrimp. In a wok or skillet over high heat, add vegetable oil and stir-fry shrimp for 1 minute.

3 Add bell pepper, carrots, mushrooms, salt, and pepper. Stir-fry for an additional minute, or until shrimp is opaque and firm. Do not overcook shrimp.

4 Remove pan from heat and stir in sauce. Transfer mixture to a serving bowl.

5 Serve by putting 2 Tbsp of shrimp mixture into each lettuce leaf, adding toppings, and wrapping like a mini burrito.

Prep and cooking time: *25 minutes*
Serves *4*

Nutrition Snapshot
Per serving (not including toppings): 188 calories, 7 g fat, 1 g saturated fat, 21 g protein, 14 g carbs, 3 g fiber, 160 mg sodium

Vegetarian

Substitute firm tofu, cubed or cut into matchsticks

Go Go Mango Chicken

Chicken is the perfect medium for a great-tasting topping. In fact, it's a little boring without it! This recipe is a favorite of adults and kids alike. Mildly spicy salsa and sweet mango chunks form a flavorful, tropically inspired partnership. Serve with Cilantro Jasmine Rice (recipe below) or a side of steamed vegetables.

- -

2 skinless, boneless chicken breasts
1 (12-oz) jar Pineapple Salsa
1 ½ cups frozen Mango Chunks or frozen Tropical Fruit Trio

1 Preheat oven to 350° F.
2 Place chicken breasts in a baking dish, cover with salsa, and top with mango chunks (don't bother thawing). Lightly drape with aluminum foil.
3 Bake for 30-40 minutes or until chicken is done and juices run clear when cut. Be careful not to overcook.

Prep time: *5 minutes*
Hands-off cooking time: *30-40 minutes*
Serves *4*

Nutrition Snapshot
Per serving (½ breast): 181 calories, 2 g fat, 0 g saturated fat, 14 g protein, 13 g carbs, 1 g fiber, 5 g sugar, 380 mg sodium

Cilantro Jasmine Rice

1 cup uncooked jasmine rice
2 cups water

½ tsp salt
¼ cup finely chopped fresh cilantro

1 Bring water to a boil. Add salt and rice. Cover, reduce heat to medium-low, and steam for 20 minutes or until water is absorbed.
2 Stir in cilantro.

Prep time: *5 minutes*
Hands-off cooking time: *20 minutes*
Serves *4*

Vegetarian

Nutrition Snapshot
Per serving: 180 calories, 1 g fat, 0 g saturated fat, 3 g protein, 40 g carbs, 1 g fiber, 0 g sugar, 291 mg sodium

Arugula Pesto Pasta

Pesto, a blend of basil, nuts, Parmesan, and olive oil, is a cornerstone of Italian cooking, used generously to add flavor to a wide variety of dishes. We use Trader Joe's ready-made pesto as a dressing in this hearty pasta salad. Chicken sausage and peppery arugula jazz up the flavors and textures.

12 oz (¾ bag) corn or brown rice penne pasta

1 (16-oz) pkg Sweet Basil Pesto Chicken Sausage, sliced

1 (8-oz) container refrigerated Genova Pesto, or 1 (8-oz) jar Pesto alla Genovese

3.5 oz (½ pkg) arugula

Shredded or grated Parmesan cheese, for garnish (optional)

1   Boil pasta in salted water, according to package instructions.
2   While pasta is boiling, pan-fry sausage in lightly oiled pan. Although the sausage is fully cooked, pan-frying imparts a nicely browned color.
3   When pasta is cooked, drain. Immediately stir in pesto until noodles are coated.
4   Toss in warm sausage slices and arugula. Heat from the pasta and sausage will slightly wilt arugula.
5   Sprinkle with Parmesan cheese.

Prep and cooking time: *15 minutes*
Serves *6*

Nutrition Snapshot
Per serving: 458 calories, 22 g fat, 4 g saturated fat, 20 g protein, 46 g carbs, 3 g fiber, 1 g sugar, 536 mg sodium

Vegetarian

Use vegetarian sausage
or omit sausage

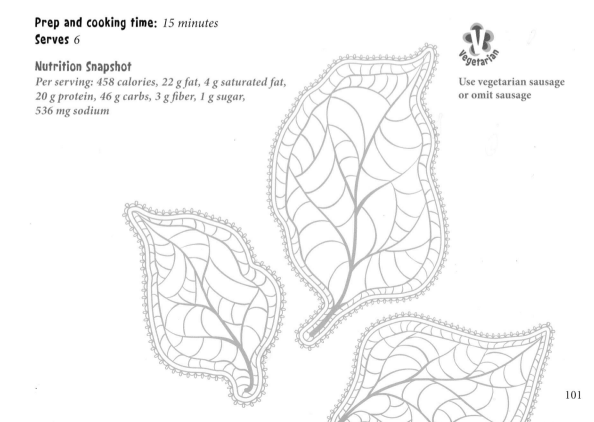

Baja Quesadilla

Don't be afraid to experiment with quesadillas. Put a little *queso* inside a tortilla, and you've got the base for mealtime creativity. Try beans, veggies, olives, chicken, marinated or baked tofu, and choose from all kinds of toppings like greens, avocado, sour cream and salsas. You really can put almost anything inside a quesadilla. A cast iron pan is nice for retaining heat and cooking a quesadilla, but almost any pan will do.

. . . .

1 brown rice tortilla

½ cup cooked chicken, such as refrigerated charbroiled Just Chicken, chopped

2 Tbsp Chunky Salsa

½ cup Fancy Shredded Mexican Blend cheese

2 Tbsp Avocado's Number Guacamole

⅓ cup chopped cherry tomatoes or chopped tomato

1 Tbsp chopped fresh cilantro

1   Place tortilla on lightly oiled skillet over medium-low heat.

2   Place chicken on one half of tortilla and cover with salsa. Sprinkle cheese liberally over entire tortilla.

3   Heat until cheese melts. Dollop guacamole inside, sprinkle in cherry tomatoes and cilantro, and fold over. Flip once with spatula to heat through.

4   Cut in half and serve.

Prep and cooking time: *10-15 minutes*
Serves *1*

Nutrition Snapshot
Per serving: 541 calories, 29 g fat, 14 g saturated fat, 34 g protein, 29 g carbs, 4 g fiber, 1 g sugar, 925 mg sodium

> **Tip:** *Don't own a pan? Don't own a stovetop? No problem! Quesadillas can also be easily prepared in the oven. Turn on your oven broiler to low or preheat oven to 350° F. Lay tortilla on a baking sheet and prepare in the same way, placing in the oven open-faced for about 5 minutes or until cheese is melted. Fold and serve.*

Vegetarian

Omit chicken

Seafood Paella

Paella is a famous Spanish dish originating from the Valencia region. This easy one-pan recipe, featuring seafood simmering in saffron rice is flavorful and festive. Pair paella with a fruity pitcher of sangria (page 220) and a few friends.

. . . .

1 cup Arborio rice, or any short or medium grain rice
2 Tbsp extra virgin olive oil, divided
2 refrigerated Garlic & Herb Chicken Sausages, sliced
2 ½ cups water
½ cup Chunky Salsa, or your favorite salsa
1 tsp Spanish Saffron (half the jar)
1 pound frozen small scallops, thawed
1 pound frozen uncooked medium or large shrimp, thawed (tail on or off)
1 cup frozen shelled edamame or peas
½ cup dry white wine

1   Heat 1 Tbsp oil on high heat in a wide deep saucepan or skillet.

2   Sauté sausage for until browned and transfer to a plate.

3   Pat scallops dry. In the same pan, sauté scallops until opaque, about 1-2 minutes, and transfer to a plate.

4   Add remaining oil to pan. Add rice and stir to coat with oil. Stir in water, salsa, and saffron to pan. Bring to a simmer and cover, reducing heat to low. After 15 minutes, when most of the water is absorbed, add shrimp, edamame, and wine, stirring slightly to combine.

5   Increase heat and simmer uncovered for an additional 5 minutes, until shrimp becomes opaque and cooked and rice has absorbed nearly all the liquid. Gently stir in scallops and sausage. Serve immediately.

Prep and cooking time: *20-25 minutes*
Serves *6*

Nutrition Snapshot
Per serving: 383 calories, 11 g fat, 2 g saturated fat, 38 g protein, 30 g carbs, 2 g fiber, 2 g sugar, 527 mg sodium

> **Note:** *Paella is traditionally made with short grain rice. Arborio is the closest to authentic paella rice such as* **bomba.** *If you prefer a light and fluffy paella, substitute long grain rice such as basmati.*

Macadamia-Crusted Mahi Mahi

This classic Hawaiian dish is an island favorite, combining nut-crusted fish with a spicy tropical salsa. Mahi mahi works well here, but you can also use halibut.

1 lb mahi mahi, fresh or frozen (thaw if frozen)
Pinch each salt and black pepper
1 Tbsp parsley, chopped finely
1 egg
½ cup macadamia nuts, chopped finely
1 Tbsp oil
1 Tbsp butter
½ cup refrigerated Fire Roasted Papaya and Mango Salsa
Extra parsley for garnish (optional)

1   Pat fish dry using paper towels. Sprinkle salt and pepper on each fillet. If using salted nuts, omit or adjust salt. Rub parsley onto fillets.

2   Beat egg in a small bowl. Place chopped nuts on a plate. Dip each fillet into beaten egg and then press both sides into nuts.

3   Place skillet over high heat and add oil and butter. When hot, add fish and lower heat to medium-high, cooking each fillet for about 2 minutes on each side, until fish is opaque and flakes easily. Take care not to overcook, as mahi mahi becomes tough and rubbery when overcooked. If fillets are very thick, preheat oven to 375° F and finish cooking fillets in oven until they are flaky. (If you cook the fish on the stovetop for longer than indicated, the nut coating may burn).

4   Top each fillet with 2 Tbsp salsa and extra parsley.

Prep and cooking time: *15 minutes*
Serves *4*

Nutrition Snapshot
Per serving: 307 calories, 21 g fat, 5 g saturated fat, 24 g protein, 5 g carbs, 1 g fiber, 3 g sugar, 358 mg sodium

Shiitake Mushroom Risotto

Risotto is a creamy rice dish made with Arborio rice. This delicious risotto is flavored with shiitake mushrooms, onion, garlic, wine, and garlic. The simple combination is fantastic without requiring heavy cream or lots of cheese for taste. Make sure that it is fluid and creamy when finished, not dry and stiff. When placed on a plate that is shaken side to side, risotto should spread and move.

- -

2 cups Arborio rice

2 Tbsp extra virgin olive oil, divided

1 small onion, diced

1 (3.5-oz) pkg shiitake mushrooms, chopped (8 mushrooms or 1 ½ cups chopped)

1 clove garlic, crushed, or 1 cube frozen Crushed Garlic

½ cup dry white wine

4 cups gluten-free chicken or vegetable broth + 1 cup water

1 sprig fresh rosemary

Parmesan cheese (optional)

1 In a saucepan, add broth and water and bring to a simmer.

2 Heat 1 Tbsp oil in a pan or deep skillet over high heat. Add onion and saute until onion begins to soften (~3 minutes), lowering heat to medium.

3 Add mushrooms and garlic, stirring and cooking for 1-2 minutes until mushrooms are soft.

4 Add remaining 1 Tbsp oil and add rice, stirring well. Continuing stirring and cooking for 3-4 minutes, allowing rice to toast.

5 Add wine and stir until absorbed.

6 Ladle in 1 cup of broth and add rosemary, stirring. Lower the heat to a gentle simmer. Continue to add broth in 1-2 ladle increments, regularly stirring and allowing liquid to be mostly absorbed before adding more. All the liquid will be absorbed over the course of 20 minutes cooking time.

7 When cooked, the rice should be *al dente* and the risotto should be fluid and smooth. Add more broth or water if necessary. Garnish with Parmesan and serve immediately.

Prep time: *10 minutes*
Cooking time: *30 minutes*
Serves *4*

Nutrition Snapshot
Per serving: 279 calories, 7 g fat, 1 g saturated fat, 6 g protein, 40 g carbs, 2 g fiber, 2 g sugar, 555 mg sodium

Use vegetable broth

Hurry for Curry

Curry sauces are complex and delicious, and they are a great way to creatively use leftover ingredients. Although bottled Thai Yellow Curry already has coconut milk in it, adding more coconut milk softens and delicately sweetens the curry. Light Coconut Milk is also easy on the calories; unlike heavy cream, coconut milk has 50 calories per 1/3 cup. Not too bad for a little added creaminess. Feel free to substitute whatever vegetables you have on hand.

1 (11-oz) bottle Thai Yellow Curry

¾ cup Light Coconut Milk (about half the can)

1 (16-oz) container firm tofu, cut into bite-size pieces

1 ½ cups green beans, cut into 2-inch pieces

1 red bell pepper, cut into bite-size pieces

½ onion, cut into bite-size pieces

½ cup baby carrots or sliced carrots

½ cup mushrooms, halved or quartered

1 Tbsp fresh basil leaves, chopped

1 Pour curry and coconut milk into medium-sized saucepan. Stir to combine.

2 Add tofu and vegetables. Bring to a boil, reduce heat to simmer, and cook 10-12 minutes, or until vegetables are crisp-tender.

3 Stir in basil and remove from heat. Serve over steamed jasmine rice or brown rice.

Prep time: *10 minutes,*
Hands-off cooking time: *10-12 minutes,*
Serves 6

Nutrition Snapshot
Per serving: 293 calories, 18 g fat, 6 g saturated fat, 13 g protein, 24 g carbs, 5 g fiber, 10 g sugar, 1067 mg sodium

Chipotle Turkey Chili

On a cold night, warm your body and soul with a big bowl of homemade chili. Refried beans thicken this version, giving it long-cooked texture and flavor in just minutes. Chipotle salsa adds a kick of heat, while a splash of barbecue sauce balances the spice with a touch of smoky sweetness.

. . . .

1 ¼ lb ground turkey (one package)

1 medium onion, chopped, or 1 ½ cups bagged Freshly Diced Onions

1 Tbsp olive oil

1 tsp ground cumin

1 (28-oz) can diced tomatoes

1 (15-oz) can black beans or kidney beans

1 can refried black beans or pinto beans (for a thinner chili, use half the can)

½ cup Chipotle Salsa

¼ cup barbecue sauce

Sour cream (optional)

Fancy Shredded Mexican Blend cheese (optional)

1 Heat olive oil in medium saucepan over medium heat. Cook onions 5 minutes. Add ground turkey and cook until brown, breaking it up as it cooks. Add ground cumin and cook 1 minute longer.

2 Add remaining ingredients. Refried beans need to be broken up and stirred into the chili until dissolved.

3 When chili comes to a boil, lower heat and simmer for 10 minutes.

4 Garnish with sour cream and cheese.

Prep time: *10 minutes*
Hands-off cooking time: *15 minutes*
Serves *4*

Nutrition Snapshot
Per serving: 387 calories, 4 g fat, 0 g saturated fat, 44 g protein, 40 g carbs, 7 g fiber, 11 g sugar, 913 mg sodium

Helpful Tip:

When cooking brown rice pasta, be careful not to overcook it, else the texture will become gummy. Drain and rinse as soon as pasta is al dente. Brown rice pasta tends to stiffen and become rubbery after refrigeration, so it is best eaten the same day.

Kinda-Greek Pasta Salad

Crunchy cucumbers, tangy feta, flavor-packed sun dried tomatoes, and briny black olives come together in a Greek-inspired pasta dish that is good cold or warm. Seasoned olive oil from the jar of sun dried tomatoes coats the pasta with more complex flavor than plain olive oil. Holistic health counselor Marcy Rosenthal developed this easy recipe; it shows how easy healthy cooking can be with a well stocked pantry and convenience items.

. . . .

1 (16-oz) bag corn or brown rice penne pasta

1 (8.5-oz) jar Julienne Sliced Sun Dried Tomatoes; do not drain oil

1 (3.8-oz) can sliced black olives, drained

1 (6-oz) container Crumbled Feta with Mediterranean Herbs

1 large cucumber or 4 Persian cucumbers, chopped (2 cups)

1 Tbsp red wine vinegar or balsamic vinegar

½ pkg (8 oz) frozen Just Grilled Chicken Strips (or grill 1 breast yourself)

1 Cook pasta according to package instructions. Rinse with cool water and drain. While pasta is cooking, prepare chicken and cut into bite-size pieces.

2 Mix all ingredients with pasta and serve.

Prep time: *10 minutes*
Hands-off cooking time: *10 minutes*
Serves *8*

Nutrition Snapshot
Per serving: 420 calories, 14 g fat, 3 g saturated fat,
17 g protein, 57 g carbs, 4 g fiber, 7 g sugar, 441 mg sodium

Omit chicken

Mediterranean Baked Fish

Classic Mediterranean flavors and colors add boldness to mild white fish in this easy entrée. Any white fish such as cod, sole, or snapper works well. White wine keeps the fish from drying out and makes a delicious sauce for dipping gluten-free bread or pouring over rice.

. . . .

1 lb (4 fillets) white fish such as cod, sole, or snapper, thawed if frozen

1 cup cherry tomatoes, halved, or chopped Roma tomatoes

¼ cup chopped Kalamata olives

½ small onion, chopped, or ½ cup refrigerated Diced Onions

2 cloves garlic, crushed, or 2 cubes frozen Crushed Garlic

2 Tbsp chopped parsley

2 Tbsp olive oil

¼ cup white wine

½ tsp salt

1 Preheat oven to 375° F.
2 Place fish in a single layer in an 8 x10-inch baking dish.
3 In a bowl, mix tomatoes, olives, onion, garlic, and parsley. Spoon mixture evenly over fish.
4 Whisk oil, wine, and salt. Pour evenly over entire dish. It won't seem like enough liquid, but more juices will be released during cooking.
5 Bake uncovered for 25 minutes, or until fish flakes easily.

Prep time: *10 minutes*
Hands-off cooking time: *25 minutes*
Serves *4*

Nutrition Snapshot
Per serving: 211 calories, 11 g fat, 2 g saturated fat, 24 g protein, 4 g carbs, 1 g fiber, 1 g sugar, 419 mg sodium

Beef Stew

There's nothing like a steaming bowl of stew or soup to comfort you on a chilly evening. Stews are popular around the globe, because the slow cook method softens inexpensive cuts of meat that would otherwise be tough. This one-pot meal takes just a few prep steps, and then you can leave the stew unattended while it simmers and fills the kitchen with aromas. You can either simmer on the stove or in the oven. Either way, the end result is a delicious, thick stew your whole family is sure to love.

. . . .

1 lb beef stew meat, or beef chuck cut into 1-inch cubes

½ tsp salt

¼ tsp pepper

¼ cup cornstarch

2 Tbsp olive oil

1 (14.5-oz) can diced tomatoes, or 1 small can tomato paste

2 cups gluten-free beef broth (use 3 cups if using tomato paste instead of diced tomatoes)

¼ cup red wine or 1 ½ Tbsp balsamic vinegar

2 tsp steak sauce

2 cloves garlic, crushed, or 2 cubes frozen Crushed Garlic (use up to 4 cloves if you like garlic)

2 bay leaves

3 sprigs fresh thyme, or 2 tsp dried thyme

1 large onion, chopped, or 1 ½ cups tiny onions

2/3 lb Teeny Tiny Potatoes, or potatoes cut into 1-inch chunks

2 carrots, cut into 1-inch chunks or ½ bag baby carrots

2 cups green beans, cut into 1-inch pieces, or 1 cup frozen peas (optional)

¼ cup chopped parsley (optional)

1   If you plan to bake the stew, preheat oven to 350° F. Heat oil in large pot over medium heat. Lightly salt meat and dredge in cornstarch, shaking off excess. Sear meat in 2-3 batches in hot oil until browned, about 1 minute per side. Browning seals in juices, for more tender meat. Don't overcrowd the pot or you'll steam rather than brown the meat.

2   Return seared meat to pot. Add remaining ingredients (except green beans and parsley) and stir. When liquid is boiling, cover, reduce heat to low, and simmer for 1-2 hours. If baking, place covered pot in oven, making sure to use an oven-proof pot.

3   Add green beans during last 15 minutes of cooking to preserve crispness. For softer green beans, add during the last 30 minutes of cooking.

4   Remove from heat and remove bay leaves and thyme sprigs. Sprinkle on fresh parsley right before serving.

Prep time: *15 minutes*   **Hands-off cooking time:** *1-2 hours*   **Serves** *4*

Nutrition Snapshot
Per serving: 283 calories, 8 g fat, 2 g saturated fat, 19 g protein, 30 g carbs, 4 g fiber, 7 g sugar, 775 mg sodium

Nutty Wild Rice Salad

Wild rice has a wonderful nutty flavor and hearty texture, making it perfect for salads, stuffing, pilaf, and soups. This entrée salad offers a symphony of textures: the chewiness of wild rice, the sweet burst of grapes, the crunch of cashews, and the crisp bite of green onion.

4 cups cooked wild rice, warm or cold

2 cups cooked chopped chicken, such as Just Chicken

1 ½ cups red grapes, halved

1 cup roasted unsalted cashews, whole or pieces

3 stalks green onion, chopped

Dressing

4 Tbsp extra virgin olive oil

1 Tbsp lemon juice

2 Tbsp white balsamic vinegar

1 Tbsp honey

1 clove garlic, crushed, or 1 cube frozen Crushed Garlic, thawed

⅛ tsp salt, more to taste

1 In a large bowl, combine wild rice, chicken, grapes, cashews, and green onion.

2 In a small bowl, whisk together dressing ingredients. Pour over salad and stir to distribute evenly.

Prep time: *10 minutes (+ 45 minutes cooking time if not using pre-cooked rice)*
Serves *6*

Nutrition Snapshot
Per serving: 468 calories, 25g fat, 5g saturated fat, 25g protein, 40g carbs, 6g fiber, 12g sugar, 325mg sodium

Vegetarian

Omit chicken and substitute edamame or feta cheese

> **Helpful Tip:**
> *1 cup uncooked wild rice yields approximately 4 cups cooked wild rice.*

Blue Corn Taco Salad Olé!

There is no such thing as a taco salad in Mexico, but this Mexican-inspired salad that uses the contents of a taco is a favorite on this side of the border. This hearty salad has plenty of crunch from warm tortilla chips and a familiar but distinctive flavor from homemade salsa vinaigrette. No need to measure any of the suggested ingredients precisely. Just improvise and throw in any salad items you have on hand.

. . . .

1 lb ground turkey or beef, cooked in 2 tsp Taco Seasoning

½ cup canned black beans

1 (7-oz) bag Baked Blue Corn Tortilla Chips

1 (9-oz) bag Very American Salad (a blend of iceberg, romaine, and red cabbage)

½ cup frozen Roasted Corn, thawed, or canned corn

1 cup fresh diced tomatoes or cherry tomatoes

½ cup chopped fresh avocado or refrigerated Avocado's Number Guacamole

¼ cup chopped onions or green onions

1 cup Fancy Shredded Mexican Blend cheese

½ cup sour cream

½ cup refrigerated Cilantro Dressing or Homemade Salsa Vinaigrette (recipe follows)

1 Preheat oven to 300° F.
2 Place tortilla chips in oven for 5 minutes to make them warm and crispy. Heat meat and black beans, either in microwave or pan.
3 Place salad in the bottom of a large salad bowl. Add corn, tomatoes, avocados, and onions.
4 Top with warm chips, meat, and black beans. Sprinkle evenly with shredded cheese. Place a big dollop of sour cream on top.
5 Pour dressing on top and toss. Serve immediately.

Prep and cooking time: *10 minutes*
Serves *4*

Homemade Salsa Vinaigrette

1 cup refrigerated Mild Salsa, or your favorite fresh or bottled salsa

½ cup olive oil

¼ cup fresh lemon juice

½ tsp ground cumin

½ tsp salt

2 Tbsp chopped cilantro

1 Whisk all ingredients until combined.

Nutrition Snapshot

Per serving: 501 calories, 20 g fat, 4 g saturated fat, 24 g protein, 59 g carbs,
9 g fiber, 8 g sugar, 711 mg sodium

Vegetarian

Omit meat or use
meatless substitute

Helpful Tip:

A cast iron skillet is one of the best multi-purpose pans to have. It's inexpensive, heavy, non-stick, retains heat well, and works great for making fajitas. Keep your pan seasoned and it will last forever.

Lime-Marinated Chicken Fajitas

Everyone loves the sizzle of fajitas and that Tex-Mex classic of onions, peppers, and juicy chicken, usually served with warm tortillas and a party of condiments. A lime juice marinade penetrates chicken quickly and adds tangy flavor that brightens the whole dish. Use Trader Joe's ready-made salsas, guacamole and selection of white and blue corn tortillas to make quick work of assembling the spread. Use leftover taco seasoning in our Taco Soup (page 63).

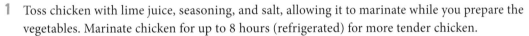

1 lb boneless chicken breasts, sliced thinly (about 2 breasts)

Juice of 1 lime

1 tsp Taco Seasoning

½ tsp salt

1 Tbsp vegetable oil

½ medium onion, sliced thickly

½ each red and yellow bell peppers, sliced, or 1 (8-oz) container pepper strips

1 medium zucchini, cut in half and sliced into ½-inch-thick spears

1 Toss chicken with lime juice, seasoning, and salt, allowing it to marinate while you prepare the vegetables. Marinate chicken for up to 8 hours (refrigerated) for more tender chicken.

2 Heat oil in heavy skillet such as a cast iron pan over highest heat. Add onion and sauté for 2 minutes.

3 Add chicken, allowing it to sear on the pan and cook for 1 minute. Add vegetables and sauté for an additional 3 minutes, or until chicken is cooked through.

Prep and cooking time: *20 minutes*
Serves *4*

Nutrition Snapshot
Per serving: 185 calories, 8 g fat, 0.5 g saturated fat, 23 g protein, 8 g carbs, 1 g fiber, 2 g sugar, 456 mg sodium

Omit chicken and increase vegetables
(or substitute tofu or soy chorizo)

Caper-lovers Chicken and Eggplant

We love easy dishes that you can quickly assemble and toss in the oven. If you love the salty, piquant taste of capers, this is a dish you have to try. Serve with a salad or a side of gluten-free pasta.

. . . .

2 boneless, skinless chicken breasts

1 Tbsp olive oil

1 medium-sized eggplant, peeled and cubed

1 (14-oz) container refrigerated Fresh Bruschetta Sauce

2 Tbsp capers

¼ cup chopped green olives

1 Preheat oven to 350° F.
2 Spread oil in bottom of 8 x 10-inch baking dish. Add eggplant to dish.
3 Bruschetta sauce will have a layer of oil on top. Drizzle chicken with this oil, coating well, and place chicken on eggplant layer.
4 Stir capers and olives into bruschetta, and spoon mixture on top of chicken and eggplant.
5 Bake uncovered for 40 minutes or until chicken is done. Very large breasts may require an extra 5-10 minutes.

Prep time: *10 minutes*
Hands-off cooking time: *40 minutes*
Serves *4*

Nutrition Snapshot
Per serving: 243 calories, 12 g fat, 1 g saturated fat, 26 g protein, 10 g carbs, 4 g fiber, 6 g sugar, 327 mg sodium

Shrimp Tacos

Soft tacos are filled with perfectly cooked shrimp, a creamy spicy sauce, and crisp butter lettuce. These shrimp tacos are so quick and easy to make, they might become a regular weeknight dinner for you. Trader Joe's Taco Seasoning Mix adds just enough kick to juicy shrimp, but – take it slow with this seasoning mix, as it is very spicy. Serve tacos with guacamole or slices of ripe avocado and tomato.

. . . .

1 (1-lb) bag jumbo or colossal uncooked shrimp such as Wild Blue Shrimp, thawed

½ tsp Taco Seasoning Mix

1 Tbsp vegetable oil

6 corn tortillas

4 Tbsp plain whole milk yogurt or sour cream

1 Tbsp Chipotle Salsa or your favorite salsa

⅓ (7-oz) bag ready-to-use butter lettuce

Fresh cilantro or parsley as garnish (optional)

1 Pull tails off thawed shrimp. Pat shrimp dry with paper towels, then sprinkle with seasoning.
2 Heat tortillas (see Helpful Tip below).
3 Mix together yogurt and salsa to create a sauce.
4 Heat oil in large skillet and add shrimp. Cook shrimp about 1 minute each side, just until opaque. Do not overcook. Remove from heat.
5 In each tortilla, add a handful of butter lettuce, drizzle with yogurt sauce, add 3 shrimp, and garnish with cilantro.

Prep and cooking time: *10 minutes*
Serves *6*

Nutrition Snapshot
Per taco: 134 calories, 5 g fat, 1 g saturated fat, 2 g protein, 20 g carbs, 2 g fiber, 1 g sugar, 45 mg sodium

> **Helpful Tip:**
> *Corn tortillas are stiff and rubbery until they are heated. An easy way to heat a large number of corn tortillas is to steam them in the microwave. First, separate tortillas from each other. Drizzle 2-3 Tbsp water on a clean kitchen towel. Fan out the tortillas slightly, wrap the towel around them, and heat in microwave for 1 ½ -2 minutes. Steamed tortillas will stay warm for 10 minutes.*

Vegetable Tikka Masala

Tikka Masala is one of our favorite Indian dishes. Masala is a slightly spicy tomato-based sauce that is commonly believed to be a product of Indian-British fusion cooking, although the origins are somewhat unclear. When you combine it with the cooling taste of yogurt, you get a Tikka Masala sauce that is nicely balanced, complex and very creamy, but not at all heavy. Try if over plain steamed basmati rice or quinoa.

- -

1 (15-oz) jar Masala Simmer Sauce

1 (12-oz) bag Cauliflower Florets or 3 cups cauliflower, cut into bite-size pieces

1 medium zucchini, unpeeled, diced into ½ inch chunks (about 1 cup)

½ cup frozen peas

¾ cup canned garbanzo beans

½ cup carrots, thinly sliced (optional)

½ cup plain yogurt, such as Plain Cream Line Yogurt

1 Pour masala sauce in a wide large saucepan over medium heat.

2 Add cauliflower, zucchini, peas, garbanzo beans, and carrots. Stir until all ingredients are coated.

3 Once simmering, cover pan and turn heat to medium-low. Simmer for an additional 12-15 minutes or until cauliflower and carrots are just tender.

4 Ladle out ½ cup or more of the curry and mix into the yogurt (this will temper the yogurt, so that it doesn't curdle in the hot curry). Stir yogurt mixture into the pan, bring to a simmer again, and then remove from heat.

Prep time: *5 minutes*
Hands off cooking time: *15-20 minutes*
Serves *4*

Nutrition Snapshot
Per serving: 175 calories, 5 g fat, 1 g saturated fat, 9 g protein, 27 g carbs, 7 g fiber, 14 g sugar, 592 mg sodium

Mini-Meatloaves

We love making mini-meatloaves using muffin or cupcake tins. This meatloaf is a new twist on an old classic. We like making them with lean turkey, but you could use beef for a more traditional meatloaf. Kids love it when we serve these at parties. While oats are inherently gluten free, they may be contaminated with wheat. Depending on your needs, use oats tested and labeled as gluten-free.

. . . .

1 (~1.3 lb) pkg ground turkey or ground beef

1 medium yellow onion, finely chopped

1 russet potato, boiled and mashed

1 Tbsp olive oil

½ cup quick cooking rolled oats

2 cloves garlic, crushed, or 2 cubes frozen Crushed Garlic

1 egg, lightly beaten

½ cup barbecue sauce

To brush on top:

¼ cup ketchup

¼ cup barbecue sauce

1 Preheat oven to 350° F.
2 Oil cupcake/muffin tins or spray well with non-stick cooking spray.
3 Sauté onion in olive oil until soft. Cool. In a large bowl, combine onion and remaining ingredients. Mix thoroughly.
4 Fill muffin tins with meat mixture, using ½ cup for each "muffin." Using your fingers, shape each one into a mounded muffin shape.
5 Combine ketchup and barbecue sauce and brush tops of muffins.
6 Bake for 30 minutes. (If you have a meat thermometer, they are done when the center measures 170° F.) When they're done, run a knife along the edge of each muffin and pop them out of the tin.

Prep time: *10 minutes*
Hands-off cooking time: *30 minutes*
Makes *8 mini-meatloaves*

Nutrition Snapshot
Per mini-meatloaf: 226 calories, 3 g fat, 1 g saturated fat, 20 g protein, 27 g carbs, 2 g fiber, 10 g sugar, 394 mg sodium

Super-Quick Mushroom Faux-Risotto

Is quick risotto an oxymoron? Not in this book. We'll make you a believer with this easy version, submitted by Susan Murai Raider from Los Gatos, California. Susan writes, "This recipe is super simple, super delicious, and healthy. My 12-year-old daughter Ruth loves this and requests it often." The trick is to use Trader Joe's fully cooked frozen brown rice. We playfully named this recipe faux-risotto because the texture isn't as creamy as traditional risotto, but our tasters gave it a thumbs up.

. . . .

2 (10-oz) pouches fully-cooked frozen Brown Rice, or 4 cups cooked brown rice

1 (10-oz) bag refrigerated Diced Onions, or 1 large onion, chopped

1 (10-oz) pkg Sliced White Mushrooms or Sliced Crimini Mushrooms

2 Tbsp olive oil

2 tsp fresh thyme, or 1 tsp dried thyme

1 cup white wine

⅓ cup shredded Parmesan cheese (preferably Reggiano), plus more for garnish

1 Heat oil in a large skillet. Add onion and sauté until soft, about 5 minutes. Add mushrooms and thyme, and continue cooking until mushrooms are soft, stirring often.

2 While vegetables are cooking, prepare brown rice per package instructions (3 minutes in microwave).

3 Add brown rice to mushroom mixture and stir. Add white wine and cook, stirring frequently, until wine is absorbed. The rice will look like risotto, although the texture will differ. Sprinkle with Parmesan cheese, stir, and cook for a half minute longer, allowing cheese to melt.

4 Sprinkle with additional Parmesan cheese if desired.

Prep and cooking time: *15 minutes*
Serves *4*

Nutrition Snapshot
Per serving: 213 calories, 6 g fat, 2 g saturated fat, 8 g protein, 32 g carbs, 3 g fiber, 2 g sugar, 128 mg sodium

Vegetarian

Chickety Chinese Chicken Salad

We dare you to try eating this dish without having the famed Barenaked Ladies tune running through your head: "Chickety China the Chinese Chicken…" This dish is as delish as it is fun, with vibrant colors and yummy peanut butter dressing. Kids and kid-like adults may not realize you're sneaking healthy vegetables into their meals. Serve this salad cold on a warm summer day.

3 cups cooked chicken, such as refrigerated charbroiled Just Chicken, cut into bite-size pieces

⅓ cup gluten-free teriyaki sauce (available at other grocers)

⅓ cup creamy salted peanut butter

1 Tbsp toasted sesame oil

⅓ cup water

½ of a red bell pepper, sliced into strips

½ of a yellow bell pepper, sliced into strips

1 cup snow peas

2 green onions, chopped

½ cup cashews

1 Whisk teriyaki sauce, peanut butter, and sesame oil until blended. Add water and mix well.
2 Place chicken, vegetables, and cashews in a large bowl. Add peanut sauce and stir to coat evenly.

Prep time: *15 minutes*
Serves *4*

Nutrition Snapshot
Per serving: 492 calories, 26 g fat, 4 g saturated fat, 40 g protein, 22 g carbs, 5 g fiber, 10 g sugar, 820 mg sodium

Egg Salad Olovieh (Persian Egg Salad)

Salad Olovieh is a Persian (also Russian) chicken, egg, and potato salad, complemented by pickles, peas, olives, olive oil, mayonnaise, and lemon. As far as egg or chicken salad goes, it's simply the best around. It's a great dish to make for large gatherings and goes over well with kids. Serve in an Udi's gluten-free bagel or on Romaine lettuce leaves.

. . . .

12 eggs
4 large Russet potatoes (about 4 cups cooked)
2 cups shredded cooked chicken or Just Chicken (optional)
2 cups frozen peas
1 cup chopped dill pickles
½ cup sliced kalamata or black olives
¾ cup mayonnaise
3 Tbsp extra virgin olive oil
2 Tbsp fresh lemon juice
Salt and pepper to taste

1 Boil potatoes (unpeeled) in a pot of water with the water 1 inch above top of potatoes. Boil for 45 minutes or until potatoes are soft when poked with a knife. Drain. Boiled potatoes peel very easily – just use your fingers to slip skin off.

2 While potatoes are cooking, boil eggs. Fill pot with cold water, add eggs gently, and place over high heat. When water comes to a boil, remove pot from heat, cover, and let it sit for 15 minutes. Drain, run under cold water, and peel.

3 Mash potatoes in a large bowl (coarsely, don't try to get it very smooth), and add frozen peas while potatoes are still hot. The heat will thaw the peas.

4 Roughly chop eggs. To the potatoes, add eggs, chicken, pickles, and olives and combine.

5 Add mayo, olive oil, and lemon juice to the mixture, stirring until mayo is evenly distributed throughout. Add salt and pepper to taste.

Prep time: *About 45 minutes of boiling (eggs and potatoes), but only 10 minutes of prep time after that,*
Serves *12*

Nutrition Snapshot
Per serving: 326 calories, 16 g fat, 3 g saturated fat, 17 g protein, 30 g carbs, 3 g fiber, 4 g sugar, 384 mg sodium

Vegetarian
Omit chicken

Did you know? *What makes some hard boiled eggs easy to peel when other times you need a hammer and chisel? For eggs that peel easily, let them stay in your fridge for 4 or 5 days first before hard boiling. Very fresh eggs are hard to peel when hard boiled.*

Salmon Nicoise Salad

Salad Nicoise (knee-SWAZ) from Nice, France is one of the many classic French dishes that Julia Child brought to America. It is traditionally made with canned tuna, but we use salmon for an up-scale touch. As a shortcut, use Trader Joe's ready-to-eat hard boiled and peeled eggs, or boil your own (see Helpful Tip on page 40).

1 lb salmon fillets
1 (5-oz) bag salad greens
4 eggs, hard boiled and peeled
1 (8-oz) bag haricots verts (French green beans)
1 lb small potatoes, such as Dutch Gold
2 cups cherry tomatoes or sliced tomatoes
1 cup mixed olives or Kalamata olives
1 (7.4-oz) jar roasted red peppers
1 (12-oz) jar Marinated Artichokes

For Dijon vinaigrette

2 tsp Aioli Garlic Mustard Sauce, or 1 tsp Dijon mustard + 1 tsp crushed garlic
3 Tbsp white wine vinegar or champagne vinegar
6 Tbsp olive oil
1 tsp salt

1 Preheat oven to broil setting. Lightly spray salmon with oil and sprinkle with salt and pepper.
2 In a large pot with salted water, boil potatoes until fork-tender, about 15 minutes. Broil salmon while potatoes are cooking, about 7 minutes, or until desired doneness. Remove potatoes with a slotted spoon.
3 In the same pot of water, boil haricots verts for 1-2 minutes. Drain and rinse under cold water to stop cooking.
4 Slice eggs in half. Arrange all ingredients on a large platter or assemble individual plates. Whisk together vinaigrette ingredients; drizzle on salad or serve on the side.

Prep and cooking time: *30 minutes*
Serves *8*

Nutrition Snapshot
Per serving: 241 calories, 11 g fat, 2 g saturated fat,
18 g protein, 17 g carbs, 5 g fiber, 3 g sugar, 474 mg sodium

Use baked tofu instead of salmon. Baked tofu is seasoned and firmer than standard tofu.

Grilled Yogurt Dill Chicken Skewers

Looking for juicy chicken and flavorful veggies? Marinate and grill them! You can use your oven or grill to make these delicious and tender chicken kabobs. For a really easy and quick meal, assemble skewers ahead of time and cover with plastic wrap. When you're ready, start some rice or pasta and toss skewers in the oven or on the grill.

. . . .

2-3 skinless, boneless chicken breasts (about 1 lb), cut into 1-inch chunks

1 cup yogurt

2 tsp dried dill

½ a medium onion, thinly sliced

½ tsp salt

¼ tsp black pepper

2 zucchini, unpeeled and cut crosswise into ½-inch pieces

1 (10-oz) container whole white mushrooms

1 large (or two small) red bell pepper, seeds and pith removed, cut into 1-inch pieces

10-12 cherry tomatoes

1   Combine yogurt, dill, onion, salt, and pepper.
2   Marinate chicken chunks in yogurt mixture for a few hours or overnight in the fridge.
3   Using long wooden or metal skewers, assemble skewers one by one, alternating ingredients. Dispose of the marinade you used for the chicken.
4   Cook on the grill or use an oven.

Oven Instructions

1   Preheat oven to 400° F.
2   Place skewers across a foil-lined 9 x 13-inch oven-safe pan.
3   Cook in the center of the oven for 15-20 minutes or until chicken juices run clear when cut.

Prep time: *15 minutes*
Hands off cooking time: *20 minutes*
Makes *ten 10-inch skewers*

Nutrition Snapshot
Per skewer: 64 calories, 2 g fat, 1 g saturated fat, 11 g protein, 3 g carbs, 1 g fiber, 1 g sugar, 90 mg sodium

Tamale Bake

Inspired by tamales, this quick and easy casserole features polenta, the Italian version of Southern grits. Polenta is firm and crumbly when cold, but is transformed into soft layers of chewy goodness when heated. Using pre-cooked polenta sold in formed tubes makes this delicious casserole a snap. Experiment with other vegetables such as butternut squash, bell peppers, or eggplant, and other cheeses such as goat cheese, to create a myriad of tasty variations.

. . . .

2 (18-oz) tubes pre-cooked polenta, each tube sliced into 9 rounds

2 Tbsp olive oil

1 large onion, chopped, or 2 cups refrigerated Diced Onions

3 zucchini squash, sliced

1 (12-oz) pkg Soy Chorizo, removed from casing, or substitute 1 lb ground meat cooked in 1 tsp Taco Seasoning

2 (15-oz) cans black beans, drained

½ cup Chunky Salsa or your favorite salsa

1 cup Fancy Shredded Mexican Blend cheese

¼ cup fresh cilantro, chopped

Sour cream as garnish (optional)

1 Preheat oven to 350° F.

2 Heat olive oil in a skillet. Sauté onion and zucchini until soft, about 5 minutes. Add chorizo and stir. Remove from heat.

3 Lightly oil a square baking dish. Place half the polenta on the bottom, overlapping as necessary. Sprinkle on half each of the chorizo mixture, black beans, salsa, and shredded cheese. Repeat with the 2nd layer.

4 Cover and bake for 30 minutes until cheese is melted and casserole is piping hot. Sprinkle cilantro evenly on top. Serve with sour cream.

Prep time: *20 minutes*
Hands-off cooking time: *30 minutes*
Serves *8*

Nutrition Snapshot
Per serving: 277 calories, 16 g fat, 4 g saturated fat, 14 g protein, 25 g carbs, 8 g fiber, 5 g sugar, 777 mg sodium

Red Curry Halibut

Halibut is a mild fish with a great texture, perfect for showing off a flavorful curry sauce. Serve with jasmine rice and Wilted Spinach (page 177). Or, if you want to make this a one-dish meal, add vegetables such as snow peas, zucchini, carrots, or whatever you have on hand. Place vegetables in the pan with fish and cook together.

· ·

4 halibut or snapper filets (if using frozen, thaw in fridge or under running cold water)
1 cup Thai Red Curry Sauce
1 Tbsp fresh lime juice
2 Tbsp chopped fresh basil
2 Tbsp chopped fresh cilantro

1 Place curry sauce in a saucepan large enough to fit all fillets. Heat sauce over medium heat until it starts to boil.
2 Add fish, spooning sauce over fillets to cover and season all over. Cover and cook 6-7 minutes or until fish flakes easily when tested with a fork. Do not overcook.
3 Stir lime juice, basil, and cilantro into sauce. To serve, plate fish and pour sauce on top.

Prep time: *5 minutes*
Hands-off cooking time: *10 minutes*
Serves *4*

Nutrition Snapshot
Per serving: 218 calories, 9 g fat, 4 g saturated fat, 24 g protein, 8 g carbs, 1 g fiber, 3 g sugar, 981 mg sodium

Lentil Haystacks

This easy dinner idea comes from Daneen Akers, author of the blog, LifewithLilybird.com. It's based on a taco salad from her childhood called "haystacks." Daneen created a healthy vegetarian version using two of our favorite time-saving products from Trader Joe's – frozen Organic Brown Rice and refrigerated Steamed Lentils, both pre-cooked.

· ·

1 (17.6-oz) pkg refrigerated Steamed Lentils

1 Tbsp olive oil

1 medium onion, chopped, or 1½ cups refrigerated Diced Onions

1-2 cloves garlic, crushed, or 1-2 cubes frozen Crushed Garlic

½ cup gluten-free vegetable or chicken broth

½ cup marinara sauce or tomato sauce

2 (10-oz) pouches fully-cooked frozen Brown Rice, or 4 cups cooked brown rice

Juice of 1 lemon

¼ cup extra virgin olive oil

Your choice of toppings – suggestions include

Feta cheese   Chopped lettuce

Avocado chunks   Persian cucumbers

Greek olives   Salsa

1   Heat oil in a skillet over medium heat. Sauté onion and garlic until onion is soft, about 5 minutes. Prepare rice while onion is cooking.

2   Add lentils, broth, and marinara to skillet. Cook until lentils are heated through and sauce is combined.

3   Assemble haystacks by putting brown rice in bottom of each bowl. Top with lentils and your choice of toppings.

4   Sprinkle with lemon juice and drizzle with extra virgin olive oil.

Prep time: *15 minutes*
Serves *6*

Nutrition Snapshot
Per serving (not including toppings): 347 calories, 13 g fat, 2 g saturated fat, 10 g protein, 48 g carbs, 8 g fiber, 3 g sugar, 290 mg sodium

Use vegetable broth

Baked Parmesan Chicken Fingers

Chicken tenders are coated with almond meal and Parmesan cheese for a tasty gluten-free crust that kids and adults will gobble up. While oven-baking won't give the same crisp texture as deep frying, it's a much healthier alternative and offers easier cleanup. Serve chicken fingers with your favorite dipping sauce.

1 (1.25-lb) pkg chicken tenders
1 cup almond meal
½ cup grated Parmesan cheese
½ tsp salt
1 tsp 21 Seasoning Salute
1 egg
Vegetable oil or canola spray oil

1   Optional step: For extra-juicy chicken, soak chicken tenders for 1 hour up to overnight in 1 cup buttermilk.
2   Preheat oven to 450° F. Line baking sheet with foil and oil generously (or use spray oil).
3   In a 1-gallon plastic storage bag, mix together almond meal, Parmesan, salt, and seasoning.
4   Beat egg in small bowl. Dip each piece of chicken in egg, and then place in bag, shaking to coat. Place chicken on baking sheet. Repeat until all pieces have been coated. Spray or drizzle chicken pieces with oil and place in oven.
5   Bake for 15 minutes, until golden and juices run clear when cut.

Prep time: *10 minutes*
Hands-off cooking time: *15 minutes*
Serves *4*

Nutrition Snapshot
Per serving: 388 calories, 24 g fat, 5 g saturated fat, 45 g protein, 5 g carbs, 1 g fiber, 1 g sugar, 552 mg sodium

Anytime Mediterranean Pasta

This pasta dish can be your fallback option any time, even if your fridge is nearly bare. Just keep a bag of corn or brown rice pasta, a bag of pine nuts, and a few jarred sauces on hand in your pantry. Parmesan cheese will keep for a long time in your fridge.

- -

3 cups (half a bag) corn fusilli pasta or other gluten-free pasta

½ cup pitted Kalamata olives

2 Tbsp Julienne Sliced Sun Dried Tomatoes

⅓ cup toasted pine nuts

2 Tbsp Pesto alla Genovese Basil Pesto

¼ cup grated or shredded Parmesan cheese

1 Cook pasta according to package instructions and drain.
2 Stir in remaining ingredients, topping with Parmesan as desired.

Prep and cooking time: *15 minutes*
Serves *4*

Nutrition Snapshot
Per serving: 368 calories, 17 g fat, 2 g saturated fat, 7 g protein, 50 g carbs, 3 g fiber, 2 g sugar, 226 mg sodium

Coq Au Vin

Coq au vin, chicken braised in wine, is a classic French comfort food rich with the flavors and aromas of red wine, mushrooms, and bacon. This traditionally time-consuming dish can be assembled quickly to simmer on the stove, using fully-cooked bacon and pre-sliced mushrooms. Using cooked bacon and skimming excess oil while simmering significantly reduces the fat in this dish while preserving the blast of flavor. Serve over new red potatoes (traditional), quinoa, or rice.

. . . .

1 (3-lb) pkg bone-in and skin-on chicken pieces (any combination of thighs, breasts, or drumsticks)

½ tsp salt

2 Tbsp olive oil

1 medium onion, sliced, or 1½ cups refrigerated Diced Onions

8 cloves of garlic (available peeled)

3 cups red wine (Burgundy, Pinot Noir, or Zinfandel)

2 cups gluten-free chicken broth

1 bay leaf

Few sprigs parsley

1 (10-oz) pkg Sliced White Mushrooms

10 slices (⅔ of a 3.25-oz pkg) Fully Cooked Bacon, or cook and drain 10 slices uncooked bacon

1 (1.5-lb) bag new red potatoes

¼ cup chopped fresh parsley

1 Sprinkle chicken with salt.
2 Heat oil in large pot or deep braising pan. When pot is very hot, add chicken skin side down. Add onion and garlic. Brown chicken for 2-3 minutes on each side. Add wine, broth, herbs, and mushrooms.
3 Cut cooked bacon into ½-inch pieces (kitchen shears work well for cutting bacon quickly) and add to pot. Reduce heat and simmer for 1 hour. Skim surface of any oil.
4 While chicken is simmering, boil potatoes until tender (about 20 minutes).
5 Remove bay leaf. Serve potatoes on the same dish alongside chicken, or roughly mash each potato once with a fork and pour chicken and sauce over potatoes. Top with a sprinkle of parsley.

Prep time: *15-20 minutes*
Hands-off cooking time: *1 hour*
Serves *8*

Nutrition Snapshot
Per serving: 305 calories, 12 g fat, 3 g saturated fat, 25 g protein, 22 g carbs, 2 g fiber, 3 g sugar, 716 mg sodium

Chicken Pesto Panini

A Panini is warm, pressed sandwich typically made with a Panini press, but don't panic if you don't have one at home. It's easy to make do by weighing the sandwich down as you cook it in a pan. The best way is to use two cast iron skillets. Place the sandwich in the larger skillet and place the other one on top. The top skillet will press the sandwich down as it toasts so the fillings melt and meld. Here we use Udi's soft sandwich bread and fill it with pre-cooked chicken, pesto, mozzarella, and sun dried tomato.

· ·

2 slices gluten-free bread, such as Udi's Gluten-Free White Sandwich Bread

1 Tbsp refrigerated Genova Pesto

¼ cup Just Chicken or leftover chicken

2 Tbsp shredded mozzarella

1   Place the bottom slice of bread in the cast iron skillet or other non-stick skillet over medium heat. Spread pesto on the slice, and top with chicken, cheese, sun dried tomatoes, and top slice of bread. Place second cast iron skillet on top to press down on sandwich.

2   Toast sandwich until golden brown on bottom. Flip, replace cast iron skillet, and toast other side until fillings are melted and sandwich is golden brown on both sides.

3   Slice and serve immediately.

Prep and cooking time: *10 minutes*
Serves *1*

Nutrition Snapshot
Per sandwich: 360 calories, 15 g fat, 7 g saturated fat, 26 g protein, 26 g carbs, 2 g fiber, 4 g sugar, 544 mg sodium

> **Tip:** *If you don't have a second cast iron skillet, simply use a brick wrapped in foil or a small metal pan weighed down by a few cans.*

Barbecue Chicken Pasta

Pasta and barbecue lovers alike will love the combination of flavors in this dish. On the surface, it may look like regular pasta and tomato sauce, but the subtle barbecue flavors play on your palate, giving this dish a great depth of flavor. If you prefer more sauce in your pasta, feel free to go heavier on the marinara or barbecue sauces. Don't skip the cilantro – it adds to the party of flavors in this dish.

. . . .

8 oz (half a bag) brown rice penne, or other gluten-free pasta
1 Tbsp extra virgin olive oil
1 chicken breast, cut into bite-size pieces, or 2 cups pre-cooked Just Chicken
1 cup frozen Melange à Trois bell pepper strips, or 1 bell pepper, cut into strips
1 clove garlic, crushed, or 1 cube frozen Crushed Garlic
1 cup marinara sauce
½ cup barbecue sauce
½ cup Quattro Formaggio Shredded Cheese
¼ cup cilantro, chopped

1   Cook pasta according to package instructions.
2   Meanwhile, heat olive oil in a large nonstick skillet over medium heat. Add chicken and sauté 5 minutes, until chicken is nearly cooked through. Add vegetables and garlic, and cook 3 minutes more. Add marinara and barbecue sauce and heat just to boiling. Remove from heat.
3   Drain pasta, reserving ¼ cup starchy pasta water to thin out the sauce. Add chicken mixture and cheese. Toss to coat.
4   Top with cilantro and serve.

Prep and cooking time: *20 minutes*
Serves *4*

Nutrition Snapshot
Per serving: 432 calories, 11 g fat, 4 g saturated fat, 22 g protein, 65 g carbs, 5 g fiber, 14 g sugar, 665 mg sodium

Omit chicken and substitute strips of baked tofu

Shrimp Mango Salad

Shrimp and langostino tails are dressed in a light citrus dressing in this colorful salad. The burst of mango flavors and creamy avocado textures jazz up this healthy version of the classic shrimp salad.

. . . .

½ lb frozen medium tail-off cooked shrimp, thawed
½ lb frozen cooked langostino tails, thawed (or 1 lb cooked shrimp, total)
2 cups mango chunks
3 oz baby spinach (half a bag)
1 ripe avocado, diced
½ cup chopped cilantro

Dressing

3 Tbsp olive oil
3 Tbsp lemon juice
3 Tbsp lime juice
1 Tbsp agave nectar or honey
½ tsp each salt and pepper

1   In a large bowl, combine shrimp, langostino tails, mango, spinach, avocado, and cilantro.
2   Whisk together ingredients for dressing. Pour over salad and gently toss to combine. Serve chilled.

Prep time: *10 minutes*
Serves *4*

Nutrition Snapshot
Per serving: 352 calories, 19 g fat, 3 g saturated fat, 24 g protein, 23 g carbs, 5 g fiber, 12 g sugar, 475 mg sodium

Helpful Tip:
Trader Joe's Just Chicken is an easy addition to any pasta salad, chicken salad, quesadilla or casserole. If you're not familiar with Just Chicken, it's just that: precooked charbroiled chicken with no preservatives or artificial additives, available in the refrigerated section.

White Lightning Chili

Hearty white chili is a tomato-less alternative to traditional chili. This sweet and spicy white chili gets its flavor and kick from Trader Joe's well known Corn and Chile Tomato-less Salsa. Quinoa is a double-duty ingredient, thickening the chili as well as adding protein, magnesium, calcium, and iron. The quinoa will absorb most of the liquid and soften, becoming a flavorful component that binds the chili together.

1 (1-lb) pkg Just Chicken (or 4 cups cooked chicken), cut or shredded into bite-size chunks

2 cups gluten-free chicken or vegetable broth

½ cup quinoa, rinsed

1 (15-oz) can white kidney beans (cannellini beans), rinsed and drained

1 (15-oz) can pinto beans, rinsed and drained

1 (13.75-oz) jar Corn and Chile Tomato-less Salsa

1 cup Shredded Three Cheese Blend for garnish (optional)

1 Pour broth into a medium or large pot. Add quinoa and bring to a boil.

2 Add remaining ingredients and return to a boil. Lower heat, cover, and simmer for 20-25 minutes, or until most of the liquid is absorbed.

3 Serve in bowls, topping with shredded cheese.

Prep time: *5 minutes*
Hands-off cooking time: *20-25 minutes*
Makes *8 (1-cup) servings*

Nutrition Snapshot
Per serving (not including cheese garnish): 284 calories, 1 g fat, 0 g saturated fat, 25 g protein, 39 g carbs, 8 g fiber, 9 g sugar, 487 mg sodium

Did you know? *Quinoa cooking instructions often recommend first rinsing the quinoa. Quinoa seeds naturally have a soapy coating that can be bitter. Processing usually removes this coating, but it varies from brand to brand, so it's a good idea to give quinoa a quick rinse before using. If the water becomes slightly sudsy, then you know that the coating was there.*

Note: *When reheating leftovers, add extra liquid, either broth or water.*

Vegetarian

Omit chicken and use vegetable broth or water

Honey Mustard Chicken

Sweet honey and tangy mustard meld in the oven to create a delicious glaze and dipping sauce. For best results, we recommend using fresh herbs. Serve with rice or mashed potatoes, and a side of steamed broccolini.

. . . .

> 4 chicken breasts or 6 thighs, bone-in or boneless
> 2 Tbsp olive oil
> ¼ cup cornstarch
> ¼ tsp salt
> ⅛ tsp black pepper
> ½ cup honey
> ½ cup Dijon mustard
> 2 Tbsp chopped fresh basil

1 Preheat oven to 375° F.

2 Heat oil in a large sauté pan over medium-high heat. Mix cornstarch with salt and pepper. Coat hicken pieces with seasoned cornstarch, shaking off excess. Brown chicken on all sides. Transfer to a baking dish. Searing chicken locks in juices and prevents meat from drying out while baking.

3 Mix honey, mustard, and basil. Pour sauce over chicken and bake for 30 minutes. Midway through the cooking, turn and baste chicken pieces once.

Substitution: *If you can get tarragon, substitute it for the basil. Called "King of Herbs" by the French, tarragon imparts a subtle licorice flavor that goes perfectly with honey and mustard.*

Prep time: *10 minutes*
Hands-off cooking time: *30 minutes*
Serves *4*

Nutrition Snapshot
Per serving: 379 calories, 13 g fat, 2 g saturated fat, 27 g protein, 43 g carbs, 0 g fiber, 32 g sugar, 715 mg sodium

Southwest Pizza

This tasty recipe combines salsa, guacamole, cheese, and cilantro for a delicious twist on traditional pizza. The dish comes together in minutes when you heat it on the stovetop and use a ready-made brown rice tortilla. The thin tortilla gets crisp and doesn't leave you feeling weighed down like some thick crusts do. Brown rice tortillas don't always work well for folded wraps and other dishes that require pliability, but used flat for a pizza, they work like a charm.

. . . .

    1 brown rice tortilla

    3 Tbsp salsa, such as Chunky Salsa

    ¼ cup Fancy Shredded Mexican Blend cheese

    3 Tbsp guacamole, such as Avocado's Number Guacamole

    1 Tbsp chopped cilantro (optional)

1 Place cast iron skillet or other large non-stick skillet over medium heat.
2 Place tortilla in skillet; spread with salsa and sprinkle with cheese. When cheese has completely melted and tortilla is getting crisp (about 5 minutes total), slide pizza onto serving dish or cutting board.
3 Dollop pizza with guacamole and sprinkle with cilantro. Cut into quarters and serve immediately.

Prep and cooking time: *10 minutes*
Serves *1*

Nutrition Snapshot
Per serving: 322 calories, 18 g fat, 7 g saturated fat, 10 g protein, 29 g carbs, 5 g fiber, 0 g sugar, 772 mg sodium

Vegetarian

Salmon Panzanella

Panzanella is a popular bread salad from Italy, originally a peasant food that has become fancy enough for restaurant menus and party spreads. It's made using day- or even week-old bread; any leftover bread such as gluten-free sliced sandwich bread or gluten-free bagel works. Never throw out stale bread again!

. . . .

1 lb salmon, cut into ¾-inch chunks

5 cups cubed gluten-free bread (day-old is preferred), cut into ¾-inch cubes

2 Tbsp olive oil, divided

Half a red onion, thinly sliced

2 cups chopped tomatoes or halved cherry tomatoes

2 cups sliced cucumbers (preferably Persian or hothouse)

1 bell pepper, cut into bite-size pieces

1 Tbsp capers, drained

¼ cup chopped fresh basil

½ tsp salt

¼ tsp black pepper

For Champagne vinaigrette
(or use ⅓ cup of your favorite vinaigrette):

1 tsp Garlic Aioli Mustard Sauce, or ½ tsp Dijon mustard + ½ tsp crushed garlic

2 Tbsp Orange Muscat Vinegar or white wine vinegar

¼ cup olive oil

¼ tsp salt

Pinch black pepper

1 Preheat oven to 450° F.

2 Season salmon with salt and pepper. Toss with ½ Tbsp olive oil until pieces are evenly coated.

3 Toss bread cubes with 1½ Tbsp olive oil until evenly coated. Place salmon, bread, and onion on a baking sheet in a single layer (or if you prefer the bite of raw onion, reserve uncooked). Bake for 10-12 minutes, or until salmon is cooked and bread is toasted. Stir halfway through baking time to roast evenly.

4 In a large bowl, combine tomatoes, cucumbers, bell pepper, capers, and basil. Add salmon, bread, and onion.

5 Whisk together vinaigrette ingredients, add to bowl, and toss until evenly coated. Allow salad to sit for 20 minutes for croutons to soak up flavor.

Prep time: *15 minutes*
Hands-off cooking time: *10-12 minutes*
Serves *6*

Nutrition Snapshot
Per serving: 364 calories, 19 g fat, 3 g saturated fat, 21 g protein, 26 g carbs, 3 g fiber, 4 g sugar, 611 mg sodium

Vegetarian

Omit salmon

Helpful Tip:
Store stale pieces of bread in a Ziploc bag in the freezer.
Use accumulated bread to make panzanella or bread crumbs.

Boursin Roasted Red Pepper Penne

Veronica O'Neill of VoKnits.com sent us this delicious gourmet recipe. When asked how she came up with it, she said it was just one of those whatever-you-have-in-the-fridge kind of recipes that she made up on the fly. Her son was very young at the time, and he liked that it was sweet and could be eaten using his fingers. Now that he's older (and using a fork), they often have it served warm on a bed of wild arugula.

. . . .

1 (16-oz) pkg gluten-free penne pasta
1 (12-oz) jar Fire Roasted Red Peppers, drained and sliced
1 (5.2-oz) pkg Boursin Garlic & Fine Herb gourmet spreadable cheese, softened
4 oz (½ block) Neufchâtel or cream cheese, softened
Dash black pepper

1 Cook penne according to package directions in salted water.
2 While pasta is cooking, assemble cream sauce. Over very low heat, melt cheeses together and blend. Be sure to use very low heat to avoid scorching cheeses. Add a ladle of boiling water (from pasta pot) to thin out cream sauce.
3 Drain pasta and add cream sauce and roasted peppers. Stir to coat evenly and sprinkle with black pepper.

Prep time: *10 minutes*
Cook time: *10 minutes*
Serves *6*

Nutrition Snapshot
Per serving: 421 calories, 15 g fat, 9 g saturated fat, 9 g protein, 63 g carbs, 4 g fiber, 1 g sugar, 272 mg sodium

Brown Butter Cod

A lemony brown butter sauce adds rich flavor to simple white fish. Any white fish such as cod, sole, striped sea bass, or tilapia will work for this recipe. Serve over Trader Joe's Garlic Mashed Potatoes, over rice, or alongside roasted vegetables.

. . . .

1 lb Alaskan Cod Fillets, thawed if frozen
½ tsp Lemon Pepper
½ tsp salt
2 Tbsp butter, divided
1 Tbsp olive oil
1 Tbsp capers
1 clove garlic, crushed, or 1 cube frozen Crushed Garlic
2 Tbsp lemon juice
1 Tbsp half-and-half
1 Tbsp chives

1 Pat fish dry using paper towels. Rub Lemon Pepper and salt on both sides of fillets.
2 Heat oil and 1 Tbsp butter in a skillet over high heat and sauté fish 2 minutes each side.
3 Transfer fish to serving dish. Remove pan from heat and add capers, garlic, lemon, half-and-half, and remaining butter. Scrape pan to loosen any brown bits and stir to create a sauce.
4 Pour sauce over each fillet.

Prep and cooking time: *15 minutes*
Serves *4*

Nutrition Snapshot
Per serving: 149 calories, 7 g fat, 4 g saturated fat, 20 g protein, 1 g carbs, 0 g fiber, 0 g sugar, 464 mg sodium

Sides

Wilted Spinach with Attitude

Remember cafeteria-style over-cooked spinach drowning in vinegar? No wonder kids hated this vitamin-packed leafy green for so many years. This version is nothing like that. It's easy to eat your spinach when it's this tasty and easy to make. Fresh spinach is cooked quickly until just wilted, preserving a vibrant green color and fresh flavor.

2 (6-oz) bags baby spinach
1 Tbsp olive oil
3 cloves garlic, crushed, or 3 cubes frozen Crushed Garlic
¼ cup water
½ tsp salt
Juice from half a lemon (optional)

1 Heat olive oil in a large pan over medium-high heat. Add garlic and fry for 30 seconds, being careful not to let the garlic brown. Garlic burns easily and tastes bitter when browned.
2 Add spinach, water, and salt. Cover and cook for 2 minutes. Lift cover and stir spinach with tongs, tossing leaves so that all the spinach wilts evenly.
3 As soon as all leaves are wilted, remove from heat. Squeeze half a lemon over spinach and mix. Serve immediately.

Prep and cooking time: *5 minutes*
Serves *4*

Nutrition Snapshot
Per serving: 54 calories, 4 g fat, 1 g saturated fat, 3 g protein, 4 g carbs, 2 g fiber, 0 g sugar, 357 mg sodium

Easy Spanish Rice

This Spanish rice recipe is so easy that you may never buy a boxed mix again. Use your favorite salsa to flavor rice with a natural combination of tomato, pepper, onion, herbs, and spices. Serve as a savory side to Mexican dishes or use as a base for paella.

- 1 cup rice
- 1 Tbsp oil
- ½ cup Chunky Salsa, or your favorite salsa
- 1 cup gluten-free chicken or vegetable broth
- 1 cup water

1 In a medium saucepan over medium-high heat, combine rice and oil, stirring until rice is coated and hot. Add remaining ingredients and stir to combine.

2 Bring to boil, cover, and reduce heat. Simmer for 20 minutes, or until all water is absorbed. Fluff with fork.

Prep time: *5 minutes*
Hands-off cooking time: *20 minutes*
Serves *4*

Nutrition Snapshot
Per serving: 218 calories, 4 g fat, 0 g saturated fat, 5 g protein, 40 g carbs, 2 g fiber, 1 g sugar, 214 mg sodium

Use vegetable broth

Coconut Curried Vegetables

Coconut milk simmers down to a creamy sauce for the vegetables in this dish. You can substitute other vegetables, such as cauliflower, green beans, or peas. Serve with any Indian or Southeast Asian entrée.

- -

3 zucchini, sliced into ½-inch or 1-inch pieces
2 carrots, chopped or cut lengthwise into thin pieces
1 red bell pepper, cut into 1-inch pieces
1 cup Light Coconut Milk (half the can)
1 tsp curry powder
1 clove garlic, crushed, or 1 cube frozen Crushed Garlic
½ tsp salt

1 In a deep skillet or wide saucepan, combine coconut milk, curry powder, garlic, and salt.
2 Bring sauce to a simmer and add vegetables. Simmer for about 10-15 minutes until vegetables are tender.

Prep time: *5-10 minutes*
Hands-off cooking time: *10-15 minutes,*
Serves *4*

Nutrition Snapshot
Per serving: 82 calories, 3 g fat, 2 g saturated fat, 2 g protein, 13 g carbs, 4 g fiber, 5 g sugar, 354 mg sodium

Oven Roasted Vegetables with Rosemary

Your kitchen is going to smell great as you roast vegetables with garlic and fresh rosemary. This healthy selection of squash, sweet potato, and red pepper is a nice accompaniment to nearly any entrée. The conveniently prepped bagged vegetables make this dish a breeze without all the peeling and chopping.

- -

2 zucchini, sliced thinly lengthwise (¼-inch thick or less)

1 cup cut butternut squash (available bagged)

1 cup cut yams (available bagged)

1 red bell pepper, quartered, with seeds and pith removed

6-8 garlic cloves, peeled

3 Tbsp extra virgin olive oil

½ tsp salt

¼ tsp pepper

A few sprigs fresh rosemary

1 Preheat oven to 425° F.
2 Toss vegetables with olive oil, salt, and pepper, thoroughly coating all vegetables.
3 Place vegetables in a single layer in a 9 x 13-inch roasting/baking pan. Make sure red peppers are cut side down. Place pan in the oven and roast uncovered for 20 minutes.
4 Add rosemary and roast for an additional 10-15 minutes or until veggies look done.

Prep time: *10 minutes*
Hands-off cooking time: *35 minutes*
Serves *6*

Nutrition Snapshot
Per serving: 122 calories, 7 g fat, 1 g saturated fat, 2 g protein, 15 g carbs, 3 g fiber, 3 g sugar, 178 mg sodium

Balsamic Roasted Fennel

The fennel bulb is the thick base of fennel stalk and is packed with antioxidants and other nutrients. Roasted fennel slices are tender, delicious, and gorgeously caramelized and browned on the edges. Roasting brings out the nutty flavor of fennel and is a perfect addition to a fall or holiday meal.

- -

1.25 lbs fennel bulbs (2 fist-sized fennel bulbs)
2 Tbsp extra virgin olive oil
2 Tbsp balsamic vinegar
Pinch salt and pepper
Parmesan cheese (optional)

1 Preheat oven to 400° F.
2 Slice bulbs into ½-inch-thick slices.
3 Place bulbs on a baking sheet (optionally lined with a Silpat baking mat) and drizzle with olive oil and balsamic vinegar. Toss to coat the slices. Sprinkle with salt and pepper.
4 Place in oven and roast for 45 minutes, flipping the slices halfway through cooking time.
5 When serving, sprinkle with Parmesan.

Prep time: *5 minutes*
Hands-off cooking time: 45 *minutes*
Serves *4*

Nutrition Snapshot
Per serving: 104 calories, 7 g fat, 1 g saturated fat, 2 g protein, 10 g carbs, 4 g fiber, 1 g sugar, 99 mg sodium

Raita (Cucumber Yogurt Dip)

Raita is a traditional accompaniment to spicy and flavorful Indian and Middle Eastern dishes. Cucumber, yogurt, and mint are such a refreshing and cooling combination. The raisins are a nice balance to both the taste and texture of this dish. Serve it as a side dish to any Indian or Middle Eastern meal.

- -

> 2 cups plain yogurt, such as Plain Cream Line Yogurt or Greek Style Plain Yogurt
> ½ cup raisins (we use Organic Thompson Seedless Raisins)
> 1 cup peeled and finely diced cucumber (2 Persian cucumbers or 1 medium cucumber)
> 2 Tbsp finely chopped fresh mint or 2 tsp dried mint
> ¼ tsp salt

1 Mix all ingredients in a serving bowl and serve right away.
2 Raita can be chilled in the fridge for 1 or 2 hours if prepared ahead of time, but it doesn't keep well overnight since the raisins swell.

Prep time: *10 minutes*
Serves *6*

Nutrition Snapshot
Per serving: 97 calories, 3 g fat, 2 g saturated fat, 3 g protein, 14 g carbs, 1 g fiber, 5 g sugar, 129 mg sodium

Give Peas a Chance

Poor green peas: always relegated to boring cafeteria fare and never invited to the fancy dinners. This recipe brings an upscale flair to English peas, combining them with crisp, flavorful pancetta and sautéed onions. Pancetta is an Italian cured meat, similar to bacon but without the smokiness. Trader Joe's sells it conveniently cubed and ready to use.

1 (1-lb) bag frozen peas, thawed
1 (4-oz) pkg Cubetti Pancetta (pancetta mini-cubes)
½ medium onion, sliced thinly
¼ tsp black pepper (optional)
Shredded Parmesan cheese for garnish (optional)

1 Heat a skillet over high heat. No oil is necessary. Sauté pancetta for 3 or 4 minutes until crisp. Transfer pancetta to a plate, leaving rendered fat in the pan.

2 In the same pan, sauté onion until soft, about 5 minutes.

3 Add peas to pan and cook only until heated through (1-2 minutes). Add pancetta back into pan, sprinkle with pepper, and toss. Transfer contents to serving bowl, and top with a sprinkle of Parmesan.

Variation: *Use crumbled bacon in place of pancetta.*
Prep and cooking time: *15 minutes*
Serves 6

Nutrition Snapshot
Per serving (not including garnish): 147 calories, 9 g fat, 3 g saturated fat, 6 g protein, 11 g carbs, 4 g fiber, 4 g sugar, 236 mg sodium

Vegetarian

Omit pancetta and instead sprinkle with Crumbled Feta, vegetarian bacon, or Parmesan to add saltiness and texture

Roasted Brussels Sprouts

We've always loved Brussels sprouts, even when we were kids. If you don't like them, chances are you've had them boiled or steamed to death. Roasting the sprouts browns them beautifully and brings out their nutty sweetness. It's an easy, elegant, and family-friendly way to serve this nutritious food. In the winter, Trader Joe's often carries huge stalks of Brussels sprouts. They are a great deal and each stalk has dozens of sprouts. Kids love breaking the sprouts off the stalk, and they will enjoy this recipe as well.

. . . .

> 1 lb Brussels sprouts
> 2 Tbsp olive oil
> ¼ tsp salt
> ¼ tsp 21 Seasoning Salute (or Lemon Pepper)
> Parmesan or balsamic vinegar (optional)

1 Preheat oven to 400° F.
2 Trim the ends of the Brussels sprouts if necessary, taking off any yellowed outer leaves, and cut sprouts in half.
3 Place the sprouts on a baking sheet (a heavy gauge restaurant-style half sheet pan works great) and drizzle with olive oil, tossing to coat. Sprinkle with salt and seasoning, tossing again. Spread sprouts evenly on baking sheet.
4 Put in oven and roast for 25-30 minutes, tossing a few times as they cook. They should be soft and very well browned when done, with some of the outer leaves crisping. Larger or whole sprouts will require an extra 10 minutes to cook.
5 When serving, sprinkle roasted sprouts with a little Parmesan or balsamic vinegar.

Prep time: *5 minutes*
Hands-off cooking time: *25-30 minutes*
Serves *4*

Nutrition Snapshot
Per serving: 100 calories, 7 g fat, 1 g saturated fat, 4 g protein, 8 g carbs, 4 g fiber, 0 g sugar, 169 mg sodium

Sweet Potatoes with Balsamic Maple Glaze

The natural sweetness of sweet potatoes is set off by the flavorful tang of a balsamic maple glaze. Sweet potatoes are tasty and easy to cook; we haven't met anyone yet, kids included, who does not love them. This delicious root vegetable also packs a nutritious punch. Sweet potatoes are full of dietary fiber, natural sugars, vitamin C, beta carotene, and vitamin A.

· ·

1 (16-oz) bag Cut Sweet Potatoes (or peel and cut your own ¾-inch cubes, about 3 cups worth)

3 Tbsp vegetable oil, divided

3 Tbsp maple syrup, divided

5 Tbsp peeled and minced shallots (~3 shallots)

2 Tbsp balsamic vinegar

¼ tsp each salt and pepper

1 Preheat oven to 400˚ F.

2 In a medium bowl, toss sweet potatoes with 2 Tbsp oil and 2 Tbsp maple syrup until coated. Transfer sweet potatoes onto a lightly oiled baking sheet. Spread them out so that they roast evenly.

3 Roast sweet potatoes in oven for 20-25 minutes, or until fork-tender, tossing halfway through.

4 While sweet potatoes are roasting, sauté shallots in a small saucepan with 1 Tbsp oil until shallots are soft. Add balsamic vinegar and remaining 1 Tbsp maple syrup. Simmer over low heat for about 5 minutes until sauce is slightly reduced and thickened. Remove from heat.

5 Remove sweet potatoes from oven and transfer to medium serving bowl. Drizzle with sauce and toss to coat.

Prep time: *10 minutes*
Hands-off cooking time: *25 minutes*
Serves *4*

Nutrition Snapshot
Per serving: 206 calories, 11 g fat, 1 g saturated fat, 1 g protein, 27 g carbs, 2 g fiber, 13 g sugar, 187 mg sodium

Butternut Squash Quinoa

Debbie Fecher from Acton, Massachusetts, sent us this recipe using one of our favorite ingredients, quinoa. Quinoa is packed with more protein than any other grain. It's a vegetarian source of the complete set of essential amino acids and is a great alternative to rice. Garlicky butternut squash complements the nutty taste of quinoa. Debbie says that her cousins ask for this recipe for all their gatherings. This dish can be served warm or cold.

· ·

1 (12-oz) pkg Cut Peeled Butternut Squash, diced into smaller pieces (about 3 cups)

2 Tbsp olive oil

½ tsp salt

¼ tsp black pepper

1 tsp garlic powder

½ cup chopped onion or refrigerated Diced Onions

1 cup quinoa, rinsed

2 cups gluten-free chicken or vegetable broth

2 Tbsp butter

⅛ cup dried cranberries (optional)

⅛ cup dried apricots, chopped (optional)

1 Preheat oven to 350° F.
2 Place butternut squash on a baking sheet. Pour olive oil over squash and toss to coat. Sprinkle with salt, pepper and garlic powder, and toss again. Spread seasoned squash in a single layer and bake for 15 minutes.
3 Add onion and bake for another 10 minutes.
4 Transfer cooked vegetable mixture to a medium pot and add quinoa, broth, and butter. Bring mixture to a boil. Cover, reduce heat, and simmer for 15 minutes, or until water is absorbed.
5 Stir in dried cranberries and dried apricots.

Prep time: *5 minutes*
Hands-off cooking time: *40 minutes*
Serves *4*

Nutrition Snapshot
Per serving: 306 calories, 15 g fat, 3 g saturated fat, 7 g protein, 37 g carbs, 4 g fiber, 3 g sugar, 573 mg sodium

Use vegetable broth or water

Black Bean and Mango Salad

Eating legumes is easy when they are attractively presented. Papaya and mango salsa brings a vibrant touch to an otherwise colorless dish and adds a fruity kick. This particular salsa is spicy – be forewarned! Substitute a milder salsa for less heat. This flavorful salad goes well with chicken or pork, and has plenty of fiber from both black beans and wild rice.

2 (15-oz) cans black beans, rinsed and drained

1 (15-oz) container refrigerated Fire Roasted Papaya Mango Salsa

3 cups cooked wild rice

1   Combine all ingredients and toss well.

Prep time: *5 minutes*
Serves *8*

Nutrition Snapshot
Per serving: 186 calories, 1 g fat, 0 g saturated fat, 9 g protein, 36 g carbs, 8 g fiber, 4 g sugar, 780 mg sodium

> **Helpful Tip:**
> *3/4 cup uncooked wild rice yields approximately 3 cups cooked wild rice.*

Roasted Asparagus with Tomatoes and Feta

Dress up asparagus with ripe tomatoes and savory feta cheese. Unlike steaming, which can yield a stringy washed-out vegetable, roasting preserves the fresh green color and crisp texture of asparagus. This colorful dish is an elegant accompaniment to any meal, especially one with a Mediterranean or Greek theme.

- -

1 (12-oz) pkg fresh asparagus spears

2 tsp olive oil

⅛ tsp salt

1 tomato, sliced

1 Tbsp Crumbled Feta

⅛ tsp black pepper

1 Preheat oven to 400° F.

2 On baking sheet, toss asparagus with oil until well coated. Line up asparagus in a single layer, sides touching. Sprinkle lightly with salt.

3 Place sliced tomatoes in a row along the center. Sprinkle feta cheese and pepper evenly on top.

4 Bake for 10 minutes until asparagus is crisp-tender. For softer asparagus, cook 5-10 minutes longer.

Prep time: *10 minutes*
Hands-off cooking time: *15 minutes*
Serves 6 *(about 3 spears per person)*

Nutrition Snapshot
Per serving: 42 calories, 3 g fat, 1 g saturated fat, 2 g protein, 4 g carbs, 2 g fiber, 2 g sugar, 71 mg sodium

Sesame Toasted Sugar Snap Peas

Sugar snap peas are delicious on their own and can be eaten raw. The less you do to them, the better, to let their crunchy sweet taste shine. Here we make the peas glisten with just a smidge of nutty sesame oil. A quick burst of heat enhances their naturally sweet flavor and vibrant color. Do not overcook.

1 (12-oz) bag Sugar Snap Peas or snow peas
1 tsp toasted sesame oil
Pinch salt
2 Tbsp water
1 tsp sesame seeds

1 Heat skillet or wok over medium-high heat.
2 Mix peas, sesame oil, and salt in a mixing bowl until evenly coated.
3 Toss peas into skillet. Add water and quickly stir-fry for 2-3 minutes until water evaporates and peas are bright green and still crisp.
4 Remove from heat and sprinkle with sesame seeds.

Prep and cooking time: *5 minutes*
Serves *4*

Nutrition Snapshot
Per serving: 49 calories, 2 g fat, 0 g saturated fat, 2 g protein, 6 g carbs, 2 g fiber, 3 g sugar, 39 mg sodium

Vegetarian

Almond Bread

Almond meal is a slightly more coarse version of almond flour, made of ground almonds with the skin left on. We use it to make delicious and healthy almond bread that is low carb, high protein, and gluten free. This bread was inspired by a recipe from Elana Amsterdam at the Elana's Pantry blog. We love the nutty taste and moist, hearty texture. Enjoy plain or topped with cream cheese and honey.

1 (16-oz) bag almond meal (about 4½ cups)

1 tsp salt

1 tsp baking soda

1 Tbsp baking powder

5 large eggs

2 Tbsp agave nectar

½ cup plain yogurt such as Plain Cream Line Yogurt

1 tsp sesame seeds (optional)

1 Preheat oven to 325˚ F.
2 In a large bowl, combine almond meal, salt, baking soda, and baking powder.
3 In a medium bowl, whisk together eggs, agave nectar, and yogurt.
4 Add wet mixture to dry mixture and mix thoroughly.
5 Pour mixture into a 5 x 9-inch oiled loaf pan and sprinkle with sesame seeds.
6 Immediately place in oven on center rack and bake for 55 minutes, or until a toothpick inserted in center comes out clean. If top begins to brown too much, drape with foil. When cool, run a sharp knife along edge of pan to loosen bread and remove to slice.

Prep time: *10 minutes*
Hands-off cooking time: *55 minutes*
Serves *12*

Nutrition Snapshot
Per serving: 317 calories, 25 g fat, 2 g saturated fat, 13 g protein, 11 g carbs, 5 g fiber, 2 g sugar, 450 mg sodium

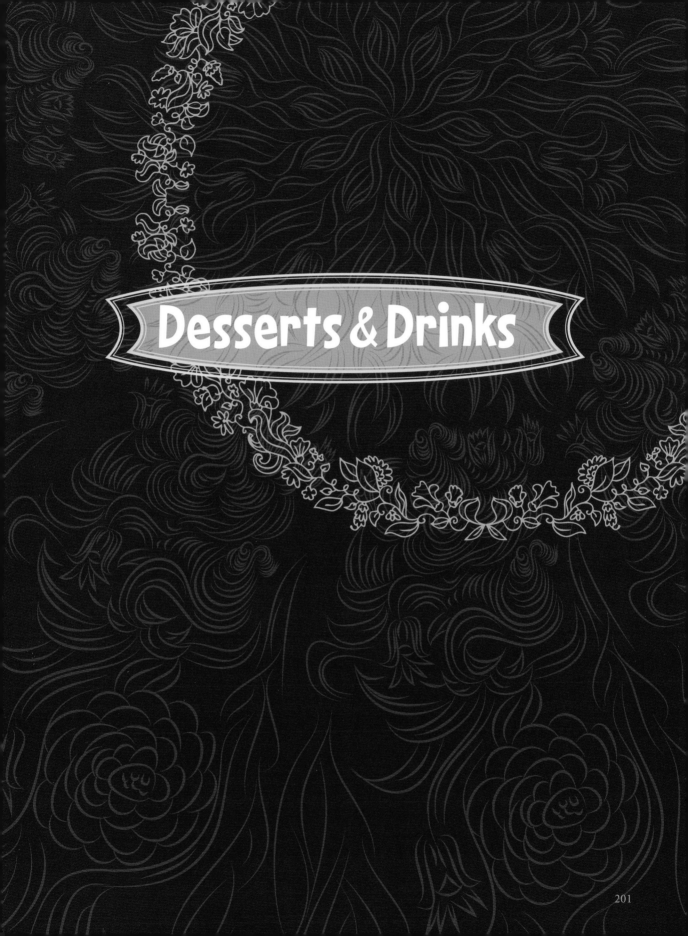

Desserts & Drinks

Berry Tart with Almond Crust

This delicious almond crust has quickly become a standard in our house given its mild, nutty taste and great texture, as well as simply how nutritious it is! Aside from being gluten free, almond meal is much lower in carbs and higher in protein and fiber than wheat flour, and it's a great source of calcium and vitamins. The crust complements any fruit, especially the tangy sweet combination of raspberries and blueberries in this quick and easy tart. Use this basic recipe as your go-to pie or tart crust (pre-bake or bake with fillings as called for in other recipes), filling it with everything from fruit to cream to cheesecake to pumpkin.

Crust

3 cups almond meal

¼ tsp salt

6 Tbsp unsalted butter
(¾ stick), melted

Filling

1 (12-oz) bag frozen raspberries

1 (12-oz) bag frozen blueberries

¼ cup lemonade or orange juice

2 Tbsp sugar

4 Tbsp cornstarch

1 pint each fresh raspberries and
blueberries (optional)

1 Preheat oven to 350° F.

2 Mix together almond meal, salt, and melted butter to form a crumbly dough. Press dough into 11-inch tart pan (9-inch pie dish is fine too. Crust will be thicker). Use fingers or the smooth bottom of a glass to press dough firmly and evenly across bottom and about 1 inch up the side. Bake for 15 minutes or until golden. Remove from oven to cool.

3 Meanwhile, add frozen berries and lemonade to saucepan. Sprinkle with sugar and cornstarch, and stir and heat until mixture bubbles. Lower heat and simmer for additional 5 minutes, stirring occasionally, until mixture is starting to thicken. Pour into crust.

4 Allow tart to cool for 10 minutes and then arrange fresh berries on top so that they settle into the still-soft filling a little (or skip this step and top with berries, ice cream, or whipped cream when serving). Refrigerate tart for 3 hours up to overnight. If leaving overnight, cover with plastic wrap.

Hands-off cooking time: *25–30 minutes*
Serves *8*

Nutrition Snapshot
Per serving: 216 calories, 15 g fat, 5 g saturated fat, 4 g protein, 19 g carbs, 4 g fiber, 9 g sugar, 67 mg sodium

Note: *Almond meal is coarsely ground almonds with the skin and results in a crust with a more rustic texture and appearance. If you prefer a crust with a finer texture and appearance, use almond flour in this recipe instead.*

Vegetarian

Orange Creamsicle Smoothie

Remember those yummy orange Creamsicles we all loved as kids? This creamy smoothie captures the orange and vanilla essence of those beloved popsicles in a healthy morning smoothie. If you don't like using ice in smoothies, or if your blender can't blend ice, simply substitute a second cup of mango for the cup of ice.

1 cup Vanilla Nonfat Yogurt

1 cup orange juice

1 cup frozen Mango Chunks

1 cup crushed ice

1 tsp vanilla

1 Add all ingredients to blender and blend until smooth.
2 Pour into glasses and garnish with an orange slice.

Prep time: *5 minutes*
Makes *2 (1½-cup) servings*

Nutrition Snapshot
Per serving: 172 calories, 0 g fat, 0 g saturated fat, 6 g protein, 36 g carbs, 2 g fiber, 30 g sugar, 52 mg sodium

Vegetarian

Note: *Vanilla Nonfat Yogurt is a sweetened yogurt. If you prefer to use plain yogurt, add agave nectar or sugar for a sweeter taste.*

Saffron Ice Cream

Something magical happens when saffron and vanilla come together. This ice cream is a takeoff of a classic Persian ice cream and is an unusual use for Trader Joe's Spanish Saffron. It's a pretty and uniquely-flavored ice cream that you'll get asked for again and again.

- 1 pint (2 cups) vanilla ice cream
- 1 tsp Spanish Saffron
- 2 Tbsp raw pistachio nutmeats, crushed or chopped coarsely

1. Leave ice cream container out until ice cream is just softened enough to stir (or microwave on defrost setting in 10 second intervals).
2. Place saffron threads in a small cup; add 2 Tbsp water and let sit for 5 minutes, stirring a little with the back of a knife or your finger until the color and flavor are released.
3. Leaving ice cream in its container, pour saffron onto ice cream and stir until color is a uniform light "saffron yellow" (don't worry if saffron threads are visible; that is okay). Add chopped pistachios and stir.
4. Put lid back on and re-freeze until ice cream sets again.
5. When you serve it, top ice cream with more pistachios.

Prep time: *10 minutes*
Serves *4*

Nutrition Snapshot
Per serving: 300 calories, 10 g fat, 5 g saturated fat, 4 g protein, 18 g carbs, 1 g fiber, 15 g sugar, 53 mg sodium

> **Note:** *You won't find rose water at Trader Joe's, but if you live near a Middle Eastern grocery, pick up a bottle of distilled rose water. Mix 2 Tbsp rose water into the ice cream along with the saffron and you will get a very authentic flavor.*

Coconut Rice with Mango

This Southeast Asian inspired dessert is a take on Sticky Rice with Mango. Our easy version uses fragrant jasmine rice, which is more widely available.

. . . .

½ cup jasmine rice
½ cup water
1 cup + ¼ cup coconut milk
3 Tbsp sugar
½ cup Mango Sauce or mango nectar (optional)
2 cups sliced mango, such as refrigerated Fresh Cut Mango or frozen Mango Chunks, thawed

1   Combine rice, water, 1 cup coconut milk, and sugar in a saucepan. Bring mixture to a boil. Reduce heat and cover. Simmer over low heat for 30 minutes or until rice is cooked. Remove from heat and let rice sit covered for another 10 minutes.

2   Drizzle 2 Tbsp of mango sauce onto each dessert plate, if using. Place a dollop of coconut rice on center of plate. Top rice with a spoonful of reserved coconut milk, letting it run down the sides. Top with a few slices of mango and serve.

Prep time: 10 minutes
Hands-off cooking time: *30 minutes*
Serves *4*

Nutrition Snapshot
Per serving: 240 calories, 4 g fat, 3 g saturated fat, 2 g protein, 49 g carbs, 3 g fiber, 22 g sugar, 1 mg sodium

Chia Energy Drink (Chia Fresca)

Whole chia seeds are combined with fresh lime juice, sugar, and water to create a chia energy drink. This ancient seed and food is high in protein, omega-3 fatty acids, fiber, and vitamins. The recipe was inspired by the book *Born to Run* in which *chia fresca* sustains the Tarahumara running people on their many-hundred-mile runs. Deana's husband swears by this drink ever since he started using chia before his triathlons and century-long bike rides. Whether you're an athlete, an Aztec warrior fueling up for battle, or just someone looking for a health boost, this drink is a delicious and easy way to add chia to your diet.

· ·

2 Tbsp whole chia seeds

2 cups water

4 Tbsp fresh lime juice

2 Tbsp sugar (or honey or agave to taste)

1 Combine ingredients in a Mason jar or small pitcher and stir until sugar is dissolved and chia is distributed in water. Chia may clump at first, so use a whisk if necessary. Taste and adjust sugar and lime juice as needed—it should have the sweet and sour balance of limeade or lemonade.

2 Allow drink to sit for 20-30 minutes or overnight in fridge until chia seeds have softened and the liquid is like a thin gel.

3 Store in fridge. Shake jar or stir as needed to re-suspend chia seeds in the liquid.

Prep time: *5 minutes*
Serves *2*

Nutrition Snapshot
Per serving: 112 calories, 3g fat, 0g saturated fat,
3g protein, 19g carbs, 5g fiber, 13g sugar, 1mg sodium

Vegetarian

Lemon Ricotta Almond Cake

This dense and delicious cake is made with almond meal, capturing the essence of classic Italian desserts. It combines the richness of almonds, the sweetness of ricotta, and the zing of lemon. Unlike finer almond flour, almond meal has a coarse grind, giving this cake a rustic texture. No other flour is used, making it healthy and gluten-free. Serve with a small dollop of whipped cream or top with extra lemon zest.

2 cups almond meal

1 tsp baking powder

¼ tsp salt

3 large eggs

1 cup sugar

1 tsp vanilla

1 (15-oz) container ricotta cheese (2 cups)

Zest of 1 lemon

Juice of 1 lemon (about 3 Tbsp)

> **Did you know?** *Almonds are a great source of protein, vitamin E, monounsaturated (good) fats, magnesium, phosphorus, zinc, calcium, folic acid and fiber.*

1 Preheat oven to 350° F.

2 In a large bowl, combine almond meal, baking powder, and salt.

3 In a medium bowl, combine remaining ingredients and mix well.

4 Add wet ingredients to dry ingredients and stir well until smooth.

5 Pour mixture into oiled 9-inch pan, deep pie dish, or springform pan. Bake 55-60 minutes until cake is completely puffed up, no longer "jiggly" in the center, and very golden on the edges.

6 Cool cake completely (it will deflate) and thoroughly chill in fridge for at least 4 hours before serving. Cake remains moist and is better the next day. Serve with whipped cream or garnish with lemon zest.

Prep time: *10 minutes*
Hands-off cooking time: *55-60 minutes*
Serves *12*

Nutrition Snapshot
Per serving: 261 calories, 14 g fat, 4 g saturated fat, 10 g protein, 23 g carbs, 2 g fiber, 19 g sugar, 156 mg sodium

Helpful Tip:

The lemon zest adds so much to this cake – choose a fresh, fragrant lemon and make sure you use only the outer peel, avoiding the bitter white pith. Use a microplane grater for tiny flecks of zest, or a citrus zester if you want larger strips of lemon as a garnish (shown in photo). Both tools are inexpensive and good additions to your kitchen drawer.

Creamy Chai

One of our readers describes chai with milk as "a warm hug," and we agree. Trader Joe's Ruby Red Chai is an aromatic blend of tea and spices, made even better with honey and almond milk. Smooth and sweet, perfect for morning or evening.

- -

1 teabag Ruby Red Chai

1 tsp honey

1 Tbsp Unsweetened Vanilla Almond Milk

1 Prepare tea with 1 cup boiling water.

2 Sweeten with honey (if desired, add more to taste).

3 Add almond milk as you would add milk to coffee.

Prep time: *5 minutes,* **Serves** *1*

Nutrition Snapshot
Per serving: 29 calories, 0 g fat, 0 g saturated fat, 0 g protein, 7 g carbs, 0 g fiber, 7 g sugar, 10 mg sodium

Mango Lassi

A mango lassi is basically a smoothie made with yogurt and mango. Flaxseed oil is optional if you want to add some healthy omega-3 essential fatty acids to your morning. Don't worry when you read the word "fatty" – omega-3's increase your body's metabolic rate, actually helping to burn excess fats in your body! You'll find flaxseed oil in the supplements section at Trader Joe's, not with the oils.

. . . .

> 1 cup frozen Mango Chunks
> 1 cup plain or vanilla yogurt (nonfat or regular)
> ¼ cup orange juice
> 1 tsp agave nectar or honey
> 1 Tbsp flaxseed oil (optional)

1 Add ingredients to a blender and blend until smooth.

Prep time: *5 minutes,* **Serves** *2*

Nutrition Snapshot
Per serving: 132 calories, 0 g fat, 0 g saturated fat, 6 g protein, 28 g carbs, 2 g fiber, 26 g sugar, 82 mg sodium

South Seas Chocolate Mousse

Tropical flavors of coconut and rum beckon the pirate in all of us. A few bites and you'll notice your guests starting off sentences with "Arrr," "Ahoy me hearty," and "T'mousse be good." The coconut is subtle and the texture is just as creamy as mousse made with heavy cream. But since light coconut milk has about one sixth of the calories of heavy cream, you won't be adding inches to your pirate booty. Sweet fruit counterbalances the bittersweet richness of the dark chocolate and add a little bit of color and flair.

. . . .

Mousse

2 (3.5-oz) bars dark bittersweet chocolate such as Valrhona 71% Cacao

1 (14-oz) can coconut milk

2 Tbsp Captain Morgan Original Spiced Rum (not regular rum)

4 oz mascarpone cheese (½ container)

Topping

2 cups diced mango (fresh or frozen) and/or fresh berries

1 Microwave method to melt chocolate: Break up chocolate bars into squares (8 squares for each bar) and place in a small Pyrex bowl. Microwave for 1 minute and stir. Repeat using 30-second intervals, stirring after every interval until fully melted and waiting a minute between intervals to let the heat of the bowl dissipate. Melting 2 chocolate bars should take about a total of 2 minutes. Be careful not to burn the chocolate.

2 Add coconut milk, rum, and mascarpone cheese to your blender. Pour melted chocolate into blender and blend right away for about 30 seconds. Pour or spoon mousse into individual cups and place in the fridge for at least two hours. If you will be leaving them in the fridge longer than a couple of hours or making it the day before, cover mousse cups with plastic wrap.

3 Top each mousse cup generously with fruit right before serving (about ¼ cup per serving).

Prep time: *5-10 minutes. Make at least 2 hours ahead of time.*
Makes *8 (½ -cup) servings*

Nutrition Snapshot
Per serving: 287 calories, 20 g fat, 13 g saturated fat, 3 g protein, 20 g carbs, 1 g fiber, 15 g sugar, 19 mg sodium

216

Basic Lemonade

We love to make this basic lemonade at home, and whenever our kids set up a lemonade stand, neighbors and passersby say that it's the best they've ever tasted. We often add a splash of rose water, which takes the lemonade to an exotic level. If you use rose water, make sure it's distilled rose water, not diluted rose oil. Any Middle Eastern grocery will have good, inexpensive rose water.

1 cup water
1 cup sugar
1 cup fresh lemon juice (about 5 lemons)
5 cups water
2 cups crushed ice
2 Tbsp rose water (optional)

1 Combine 1 cup water and sugar in a saucepan over medium-low heat and stir until sugar dissolves. Remove from heat. This is your sugar syrup.

2 In a pitcher or other container, combine sugar syrup, lemon juice, 5 cups water, ice, and rose water.

3 Taste and adjust for sweetness.

Prep time: *10 minutes,* **Serves** *10*

Nutrition Snapshot
Per serving: 83 calories, 0 g fat, 0 g saturated fat, 0 g protein, 22 g carbs, 0 g fiber, 21 g sugar, 5 mg sodium

Honey Mint Fruit Salad

For a light finish to any meal, try a fruit salad made with fresh fruits in season. Choose any combination of fruits such as strawberries, blueberries, melon balls, kiwi, and grapes. Brighten up the flavors with a touch of honey, mint, and lime.

- -

1 heaping cup of fruits in season, cut in large pieces
1 tsp chopped mint leaves (a few leaves)
1 tsp lime juice
1 tsp honey

1 To make dressing, mix together mint leaves, honey, and lime juice.
2 Place fruits in a bowl and drizzle with dressing.

Prep time: *5-10 minutes*
Serves *1*

Nutrition Snapshot
*Per serving: 131 calories, 1 g fat,
0 g saturated fat, 2 g protein,
33 g carbs, 4 g fiber, 27 g sugar,
25 mg sodium*

Sangria

Sangria is a delicious and easy Spanish wine and fruit punch. It is traditionally made with Bordeaux wine, although the idea has been adapted to all kinds of wines and fruits. Even if you have friends who aren't "wine people," there's a good chance they'll like sangria. Serve sangria in a pitcher as a party drink, a summertime punch, or as a perfect accompaniment to our Seafood Paella (page 105).

. . . .

1 bottle red wine

1 lime, cut in thin slices

1 orange, cut in thin slices

1 apple, cut in thin slices

1 cup cold French Market Lemonade or other fizzy lemon/lime soda

1 Combine wine and fruits in a clear glass pitcher, and place in fridge for at least one hour.

2 Add lemonade or soda just before serving.

Prep time: *10 minutes*

Serves *4*

Nutrition Snapshot

Per serving: 229 calories, 0 g fat, 0 g saturated fat, 1 g protein, 25 g carbs, 2 g fiber, 8 g sugar, 7 mg sodium

Balsamic Strawberries

Balsamic vinegar intensifies the sweetness of strawberries, so you can enjoy this dessert even when strawberries aren't at their best. Don't be afraid of the vinegar – it truly adds a layer of flavor to the strawberries and brings out their natural sweetness. Serve over vanilla bean ice cream.

- -

2 cups sliced strawberries
1 Tbsp balsamic vinegar
2 Tbsp sugar
¼ cup red wine

1 Place balsamic vinegar, sugar, and wine into a saucepan. Heat until boiling, then reduce heat and simmer for 5 minutes, stirring occasionally. Let cool slightly.
2 Place strawberries in a glass bowl. Pour balsamic syrup over berries and stir to coat. Let marinate for 15 minutes but no longer than 30 minutes, or strawberries will be cooked from the vinegar's acidity.

Prep time: *5 minutes (not counting marinating time)*
Cook time: *5 minutes*
Serves *4*

Nutrition Snapshot
Per serving: 60 calories, 0 g fat, 0 g saturated fat, 0.5 g protein, 14 g carbs, 2 g fiber, 11 g sugar, 2 mg sodium

Note: *If preparing in advance, combine prepared syrup and strawberries 15-30 minutes before serving.*

Chocolate Coffee Fudge

This rich fudge is ridiculously easy -- only 3 ingredients and a few minutes to prepare. Wona sent this fudge to her husband's office for a chocolate-themed contest, and it won, beating out a multitude of extravagant, complex desserts. When she was asked for the recipe, she was almost embarrassed to share it given how simple it is! A hint of coffee enhances the taste of the chocolate and adds complexity to the fudge. Try adding a small amount of instant coffee the next time you make a chocolate dessert.

1 (14-oz) can sweetened condensed milk
2 Tbsp instant coffee
½ Tbsp water
1 (12-oz) bag semi-sweet chocolate chips

1 Heat condensed milk in a heavy saucepan over medium heat.
2 Dissolve instant coffee in water (it will be thick) and stir into condensed milk.
3 Add chocolate chips, reduce flame to low, and stir until melted and smooth. Be careful not to scorch fudge.
4 Pour into an oiled 8x8-inch pan. Chill in fridge until set, about 2 hours.

Prep time: *5-10 minutes*
Makes *about 20 small pieces*

Nutrition Snapshot
Per piece: 154 calories, 6 g fat, 4 g saturated fat, 3 g protein, 23 g carbs, 1 g fiber, 20 g sugar, 20 mg sodium

Tip: *When cutting fudge, a plastic knife is easiest. If using a regular knife, wipe it clean in between cuts. Then use a spatula to lift out pieces. You can also line pan with wax paper for easier removal.*

Vegetarian

Sunflower Butter Cookies

These easy sunflower butter cookies are a tasty variation on traditional peanut butter cookies. They're sweet, dense, nutty, and slightly chewy, just the way these cookies should be. Sunflower butter is an alternative for people who are allergic to peanut butter or simply prefer its taste. If you want to stick with tradition, peanut butter will work just as well.

1 (16-oz) jar Sunflower Butter (about 1¾ cups) at room temperature

1 cup sugar

2 eggs

1 tsp vanilla

1 pinch salt

1 In a medium bowl, mix together sunflower butter, sugar, eggs, vanilla, and salt until smooth. Dough will slightly thicken after being mixed together.

2 Refrigerate for about 1 hour.

3 Preheat oven to 350˚ F.

4 Scoop walnut-size portions of dough, lightly roll in hands, and place on a lightly oiled or lined baking heet (Silpat baking mats work well). Dough will be soft but holds together without being sticky. Place cookies about 1-2 inches apart, as they will not spread much.

5 Make imprints on top of cookies with a fork. If the fork sticks, dip fork in sugar or sprinkle a tiny bit of sugar on each cookie before pressing fork into it.

6 Bake for 12 minutes. Don't overbake these cookies! Allow cookies to cool before removing from baking sheet.

Prep time: *10 minutes*
Hands-off cooking time: *12 minutes*
Makes *30 cookies*

Nutrition Snapshot
Per cookie: 116 calories, 8 g fat, 1 g saturated fat, 4 g protein, 10 g carbs, 2 g fiber, 8 g sugar, 65 mg sodium

Note: *Sunflower butter turns dark green when the naturally occurring chlorogenic acid (a desirable antioxidant) in sunflower seeds meets baking soda. These cookies don't contain baking soda, so they won't turn green, but you will notice the effect in recipes that do, a great coincidence when baking for holidays like St. Patrick's.*

Chocolate Almond Cookies

Wanda Beaver makes these sensational cookies at her bakery in Toronto, Wanda's Pie in the Sky. We were delighted when she granted us permission to reprint her recipe. These wonderfully chewy, gorgeous little morsels are loaded with chocolate and finely ground almonds, giving then the texture and flavor of chocolate marzipan. Crisp on the outside, chewy moist on the inside - these cookies are utterly irresistible.

. . . .

8 oz. semisweet chocolate, chopped, or chocolate chips

2 Tbsp. butter

1 ¼ cups almond meal or finely ground almonds

2 eggs

¾ cup sugar

1 tsp vanilla

¼ tsp almond extract

½ cup powdered sugar, sifted (optional)

1 Melt chocolate and butter in microwave or in a double boiler, stirring until smooth. Add almonds and stir until combined.

2 Using an electric mixer or whisk, beat eggs, sugar, vanilla, and almond extract until light and fluffy. Add chocolate mixture and fold in thoroughly. Chill for at least 1 hour.

3 Preheat oven to 350°F. Line two 18x12-inch baking sheets with parchment paper or Silpat nonstick mats.

4 Form dough into 1-inch balls and roll them in powdered sugar. Place 2 inches apart on prepared pans. Work quickly so the dough remains cold.

5 Bake for 10 to 12 minutes. Cookies will puff slightly and the surface will crack. Cool on pans. Store in a tightly closed container up to 1 week.

Prep time: *20 minutes (not including 1 hour chill time)*
Hands-off cooking time: *10-12 minutes*
Makes *18 cookies*

Nutrition Snapshot
Per cookie: 164 calories, 10 g fat, 4 g saturated fat, 3 g protein, 18 g carbs, 1 g fiber, 15 g sugar, 10 mg sodium

Vegetarian

Almond Pudding

You may never have had a pudding like this before, made only with almond meal and no rice or wheat. A touch of Italian and a touch of Turkish, this pudding is flavored with the great taste and texture of ground almonds and subtle hints of coffee, cinnamon, and vanilla. Some claim it's perfect for an indulgent breakfast! Top with whipped cream, Organic Apricot Orange Fruit Spread, or enjoy plain.

2 cups almond meal

4 cups whole milk

1 cup sugar

1 tsp cinnamon

1 tsp instant coffee

1 tsp pure vanilla extract

1 Mix all the ingredients in a medium saucepan over medium heat and stir until smooth.
2 As it just begins to simmer, turn heat to low and continue stirring occasionally for 20 minutes, making sure pudding is not sticking to sides or bottom.
3 Pour into 8 small bowls or cups and chill in the fridge for a couple of hours until set. If leaving overnight, cover with plastic wrap.

Cooking time: *25 minutes*
Serves *8*

Nutrition Snapshot
Per serving: 354 calories, 19 g fat, 3 g saturated fat, 11 g protein, 37 g carbs, 3 g fiber, 32 g sugar, 49 mg sodium

Vegetarian

Baked Pearfection

Baked pears are an elegant dessert, rich with aromas of vanilla, honey, and spice. It's traditional to bake pears in Brandy, but here we use Drambuie, a scotch whisky liqueur from the Isle of Skye. Drambuie is sweet, infused with spices and herbs, and adds depth of flavor to the pears and sauce. If you don't have Drambuie, substitute brandy for the classic version of this dessert.

2 pears (Bosc are best for baking, but most pears in season will work)
1 Tbsp butter
2 Tbsp honey
1 tsp vanilla
2 Tbsp Drambuie
¼ cup Candied Pecans or Candied Walnuts (optional)

1 Preheat oven to 375° F.
2 Peel and halve pears. Use a spoon to remove cores. Arrange pear halves, cut side up, on an oven safe dish.
3 In a small saucepan over medium heat, combine butter, honey, vanilla, and Drambuie. When mixture is warm and butter has melted, remove from heat. Brush mixture onto all sides of each pear half, and then pour mixture onto pears, letting excess liquid run off sides into baking dish. Set saucepan aside for further use. Drape baking dish with foil and bake pears for 20 minutes.
4 Plate pears, leaving any liquid in baking dish. Pour liquid into the same saucepan and reduce over medium-low heat for 5 minutes until liquid is syrupy.
5 When serving, sprinkle with a few pecans and spoon syrup over each pear.

Prep time: *10 minutes*
Hands-off cooking time: *20 minutes*
Serves *4*

Nutrition Snapshot
Per serving (not including nuts): 129 calories, 3 g fat, 2 g saturated fat, 0 g protein, 23 g carbs, 3 g fiber, 21 g sugar, 2 mg sodium

Vegetarian

Helpful Tip:
When brushing butter or sauces, use a silicone brush. Unlike traditional pastry brushes, silicone brushes are easy to clean and won't fray or get gunky over time.

Nearly Instant Homemade Mango Ice Cream

Yes, it's possible to make ice cream at home without an ice cream maker and in just minutes! The trick is to combine frozen fruit and half-and-half (or heavy cream) in a food processor. The result is a soft ice cream, made with any fruit flavor you like. Although the texture is not identical to commercial ice cream, the flavor is outstanding, and it just can't get simpler to make ice cream.

. . . .

12 oz (about half the bag) Frozen Mango Chunks
⅔ cup half-and-half
¼ cup sugar

1 Combine half-and-half and sugar and stir for 30 seconds until sugar starts to dissolve.
2 Do not thaw mango; for this recipe it should be frozen hard. Add frozen mango to a food processor, and process just to chop it up roughly. Add half-and-half and process until mixture is smooth (1-2 minutes).
3 Serve right away. Or, for a hard-frozen ice cream, pour into a freezer-safe container and place in freezer for about 2 hours. Stir it every 30 minutes until it freezes, helping to break up ice crystals that may form.

Variation: *Use frozen strawberries or any other frozen fruit instead of mango. Experiment with unusual fruits and combinations for unique ice creams all your own! For a richer ice cream, substitute heavy cream.*

Prep time: *5 minutes*
Makes *4 (½-cup) servings*

Nutrition Snapshot
Per serving: 157 calories, 5 g fat, 3 g saturated fat, 2 g protein, 27 g carbs, 1 g fiber, 21 g sugar, 17 mg sodium

Chocolate Bread Pudding

Gluten-free doesn't mean saying goodbye to favorite desserts such as bread pudding. This four-ingredient bread pudding takes advantage of Trader Joe's gluten-free brownie mix and Udi's wonderful gluten-free bread to create a rich, warm, gooey bread pudding perfect with ice cream, whipped cream, or caramel sauce.

. . . .

7 cups cubed Udi's Gluten-Free White Sandwich Bread (about 10 slices)*
1 ¼ cups Gluten-Free Brownie Baking Mix
2 cups whole milk
1 large egg

1 Place cubed bread in large bowl.
2 In a separate bowl, whisk together brownie mix, milk, and egg. Pour mixture over cubed bread. Allow bread to absorb liquid for at least 30 minutes up to overnight. (Alternatively, prepare in the morning and refrigerate until ready to bake at dinnertime). If necessary, gently stir once or twice to redistribute liquid.
3 Preheat oven to 350° F. Transfer mixture to oiled 8x8-inch baking dish and use a spatula to compact lightly. Lightly drape with foil and bake for 45 minutes or until knife inserted in center comes out clean.

Prep time: *10 minutes*
Hands-off Cooking Time: *45 minutes*
Serves *9*

Nutrition Snapshot
Per serving: 214 calories, 5 g fat, 1 g saturated fat, 6 g protein, 37 g carbs, 2 g fiber, 18 g sugar, 284 mg sodium

*Note: *Other brands of gluten-free breads may have denser textures. Allow mixture to soak overnight so cubed bread is soaked through.*

Bellini

The Bellini is one of Italy's most popular cocktails, originating in Venice. Traditionally made with Prosecco sparkling wine and white peach purée, it's a refreshing, fruity, and light drink perfect for summer days and celebrations. We use peach juice, conveniently adding summer sweetness.

. . . .

²/₃ **cup Prosecco, chilled**

¹/₃ **cup Dixie Peach juice or other peach nectar, chilled**

1 Add peach juice to highball glasses or champagne flutes.
2 Add Prosecco and serve immediately. Do not stir or the drink will fall flat.

Prep time: *2 minutes*
Serves *1*

Nutrition Snapshot
Per serving: 85 calories, 0 g fat, 0 g saturated fat, 0 g protein, 11 g carbs, 0 g fiber, 10 g sugar, 9 mg sodium

Note: *1 bottle of Prosecco serves 4*

Vegetarian

Breakfast

Super-Food Fruit Smoothie

We love a good smoothie as a healthful and easy way to start the day. For the most part, we tend to make them with ingredients on hand, but we've found a few favorites we repeat again and again. Kids love smoothies too, and it's an easy way to experiment with healthy additions. This particular smoothie is primarily made of fruit and yogurt but has a few additions that round it out. The protein in tofu and yogurt balances the fruit carbohydrates. Flax oil is a viable source of essential fatty acids, and Very Green powder packs a punch of vegetable minerals, vitamins, enzymes, and antioxidants.

1 ripe banana, peeled

1 cup plain yogurt

½ cup frozen blueberries

1 cup frozen Mango Chunks

⅓ cup soft/regular tofu (about a ¾-inch slice off the end)

1 Tbsp Very Green powdered supplement

2 Tbsp flax oil

1 Tbsp honey

½ cup almond milk or milk of your choice.

1 Add all ingredients to a blender. Blend for a couple of minutes or until smooth.

2 For a delicious smoothie bowl with a little added crunch, pour in a bowl and top with a few Tbsp of gluten-free granola and some fresh berries.

Prep time: *10 minutes*
Serves *4*

Nutrition Snapshot
Per serving: 219 calories, 9 g fat, 1 g saturated fat, 8 g protein, 29 g carbs, 2 g fiber, 21 g sugar, 59 mg sodium

Vegetarian

> **Tip:** *If you have a popsicle mold, a great way to use leftover smoothies is to make smoothie pops. It's a big hit on summer days!*

Dairy-Free Creamy Cashew Smoothie

It's hard to believe there aren't any dairy products in this creamy smoothie. The texture of this fruit and nut-based drink comes from cashew butter. And if you're watching your waist, don't be afraid—cashews are nuts with lower fat content. Furthermore, most of the fat in cashews is oleic acid, which is a heart-healthy monounsaturated fatty acid. Cashews are also a great source of copper, manganese, phosphorus, and magnesium! Mangoes, papaya, and banana are all high in potassium and antioxidant vitamins A and C, and studies show that dates are one of the highest sources of antioxidants.

. . . .

1 ripe banana, peeled

2 heaping cups frozen Tropical Fruit Trio or Mango Chunks

1½ cups almond milk or milk of your choice

½ cup cashew butter

2 very soft dates, pitted (optional, don't use if they are very dry)

1 Add all ingredients to a blender.
2 Blend for a couple of minutes or until smooth.

Prep time: *10 minutes*
Serves *4*

Nutrition Snapshot
Per serving: 325 calories, 16 g fat, 3 g saturated fat, 6 g protein, 44 g carbs, 6 g fiber, 28 g sugar, 63 mg sodium

Swiss Muesli

Muesli was first introduced in 1900 by a Swiss physician who served it in his hospital as part of a healthy diet for his patients. Believe us, this tastes nothing like hospital food! Fresh oats are soaked overnight, combined with crisp apples and nuts for a truly satisfying breakfast. Full of whole grains, calcium, vitamins, and fiber, this is a power-packed breakfast that gets your day started right. What a bonus that it tastes great too.

2 cups gluten-free rolled oats

2 cups skim, lowfat, or whole milk, soy milk, or almond milk

½ cup orange juice (optional)

1 cup lowfat or whole plain yogurt

2 Tbsp honey

1 crisp apple, chopped in small pieces (keep the peel on for extra fiber)

⅓ cup sliced almonds

1 Whisk milk, orange juice, yogurt, and honey in a glass bowl.

2 Stir in oats, apples, almonds, and raisins.

3 Soak overnight in refrigerator to allow oats to soften. Muesli will be thick after soaking, and can be thinned with additional milk before serving.

Prep time: *10 minutes*
Serves *8*

Nutrition Snapshot
Per serving: 80 calories, 2 g fat, 0 g saturated fat, 3 g protein, 13 g carbs, 1 g fiber, 5 g sugar, 25 mg sodium

Note: *If cross-contamination is a concern, use oats that have been tested and labeled gluten free.*

Hey Huevos Rancheros

Amigo, do you like a breakfast with more of a kick? Spice things up with this satisfying Mexican-style egg dish. On the side, serve black beans topped with a dollop of yogurt, slices of avocado and tomato, or fresh fruit.

. . . .

2 eggs

2 small corn tortillas

Salt to taste

1 Tbsp guacamole, such as Avocado's Number Guacamole

1 Tbsp salsa, such as Chunky Salsa

1 Tbsp yogurt or sour cream

1 Warm tortillas in a pan and set aside.

2 Heat a lightly oiled nonstick skillet over medium-high heat. Gently crack eggs into pan, taking care to keep yolks whole. Sprinkle with a pinch of salt. Decrease heat to low and cover pan. Cook eggs only until whites are set and yolk has thickened but is not yet hard.

3 Place one egg inside each tortilla, topping with guacamole, salsa, and yogurt.

Prep time and cooking time: *5-10 minutes*
Serves *1*

Nutrition Snapshot
Per serving: 352 calories, 15 g fat, 4 g saturated fat, 18 g protein, 34 g carbs, 5 g fiber, 5 g sugar, 410 mg sodium

Purple Porridge

With a touch of vanilla and cinnamon, this oatmeal is naturally sweetened with banana. Sweet blueberries turn the porridge purple, appealing to kids (or the kid in all of us). Fresh blueberries can be substituted, but the intense color is most easily released by frozen blueberries. As an added bonus, extra frozen blueberries can be stirred in right before eating as a way to cool a steaming bowl of porridge quickly! Banana provides plenty of natural sweetness, but a little bit of maple syrup, agave nectar, honey, or sweetened almond milk can be added for an even sweeter taste.

- -

½ cup Quick Cook Steel Cut Oats

1 ½ cup water

1 ripe banana, chopped

1 tsp vanilla

Sprinkle of cinnamon

½ cup frozen blueberries

1 Add all ingredients to a small saucepan. Bring to a boil and reduce to a simmer. Cook for 5-7 minutes, or until water is absorbed.

2 Serve with milk, drizzling maple syrup, agave nectar, or honey on top as desired.

Prep and cooking time: *10 minutes*
Serves *2*

Nutrition Snapshot
Per serving: 235 calories, 3 g fat, 1 g saturated fat, 6 g protein, 46 g carbs, 6 g fiber, 12 g sugar, 1 mg sodium

Note: *If cross-contamination is a concern, use oats that have been tested and labeled gluten free.*

Vegetarian

Mushroom Basil Frittata

A frittata is similar to a quiche, but without the crust. You can use virtually any ingredients you have on hand—it's a great way to use leftover veggies. This version uses criminis, which are actually baby Portobello mushrooms. They have more flavor and nutrients than standard mushrooms, but for a milder flavor, you can use white button mushrooms or another variety of your choice. This versatile dish can be served around the clock. It's great for breakfast with a warm mug of coffee, or for dinner with a green salad.

3 cups fresh Sliced Crimini Mushrooms

3 Tbsp butter

8 eggs

⅓ cup whole milk or heavy cream

½ tsp salt

¼ tsp black pepper

½ cup fresh basil leaves, roughly chopped

½ cup Quattro Formaggio shredded cheese

1 Preheat oven to 350° F.
2 Melt butter in a 10-inch nonstick oven-safe skillet over medium heat. Add mushrooms and cook for 5 minutes.
3 While mushrooms are cooking, whisk eggs, milk, salt, and pepper until combined. Mix in basil and cheese.
4 Pour egg mixture into hot skillet, over the cooked mushrooms. Place in oven for 30 minutes or until egg is set. Eggs will puff up while cooking but will deflate when you take it out of the oven.

Prep time: *10 minutes*
Hands-off cooking time: *30 minutes*
Serves *6*

Nutrition Snapshot
Per serving: 235 calories, 20 g fat, 10 g saturated fat, 12 g protein, 3 g carbs, 0 g fiber, 1 g sugar, 368 mg sodium

Quick and Creamy Quinoa Cereal

Quinoa (pronounced KEEN-wah) is a nice alternative to oatmeal in the morning; just a little bit is very satisfying. High in protein and gluten free, quinoa is super healthy and has a nice "seedy" texture and a nutty taste. Start with our recipe below and then experiment with your own additions.

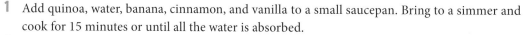

1 cup uncooked quinoa, rinsed and drained

2 cups water

½ tsp cinnamon

½ tsp vanilla extract or flavoring

1 ripe banana, peeled and diced

½ cup dried Golden Berry Blend or Dried Berry Medley

¼ cup slivered almonds

1 Add quinoa, water, banana, cinnamon, and vanilla to a small saucepan. Bring to a simmer and cook for 15 minutes or until all the water is absorbed.

2 Mix in nuts and dried berries. Top with cream, milk, honey, Turbinado sugar, or maple syrup as desired.

Prep time: *5 minutes*
Hands-off cooking time: *15 minutes*
Serves *4*

Nutrition Snapshot
Per serving: 315 calories, 7 g fat, 0 g saturated fat, 8 g protein, 58 g carbs, 6 g fiber, 21 g sugar, 5 mg sodium

Recipe Index

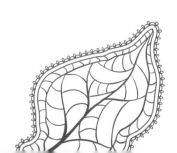

Vegetarian Recipes Index

Recipes that are Vegetarian or can easily be made Vegetarian (*) using simple substitutions

Vegetarian Recipes Index (cont.)

Recipes that are Vegetarian or can easily be made Vegetarian (*) using simple substitutions

Trader Joe's Store Locations

Arizona

Ahwatukee # 177
4025 E. Chandler Blvd., Ste. 38
Ahwatukee, AZ 85048
Phone: 480-759-2295

Glendale # 085
7720 West Bell Road
Glendale, AZ 85308
Phone: 623-776-7414

Mesa # 089
2050 East Baseline Rd.
Mesa, AZ 85204
Phone: 480-632-0951

Paradise Valley # 282
4726 E. Shea Blvd.
Phoenix, AZ 85028
Phone: 602-485-7788

**Phoenix
(Town & Country) # 090**
4821 N. 20th Street
Phoenix, AZ 85016
Phone: 602-912-9022

Prescott
252 Lee Blvd
Prescott, AZ 86303
Phone: 928-443-9075

Scottsdale (North) # 087
7555 E. Frank Lloyd Wright
N. Scottsdale, AZ 85260
Phone: 480-367-8920

Scottsdale # 094
6202 N. Scottsdale Road
Scottsdale, AZ 85253
Phone: 480-948-9886

Surprise # 092
14095 West Grand Ave.
Surprise, AZ 85374
Phone: 623-546-1640

Tempe # 093
6460 S. McClintock Drive
Tempe, AZ 85283
Phone: 480-838-4142

**Tucson
(Crossroads) # 088**
4766 East Grant Road
Tucson, AZ 85712
Phone: 520-323-4500

**Tucson (Wilmot &
Speedway)# 095**
1101 N. Wilmot Rd.
Suite #147
Tucson, AZ 85712
Phone: 520-733-1313

**Tucson (Campbell &
Limberlost) # 191**
4209 N. Campbell Ave.
Tucson, AZ 85719
Phone: 520-325-0069

Tucson - Oro Valley # 096
7912 N. Oracle
Oro Valley, AZ 85704
Phone: 520-797-4207

California

Agoura Hills
28941 Canwood Street
Agoura Hills, CA 91301
Phone: 818-865-8217

Alameda # 109
2217 South Shore Center
Alameda, CA 94501
Phone: 510-769-5450

Aliso Viejo # 195
The Commons
26541 Aliso Creek Road
Aliso Viejo, CA 92656
Phone: 949-643-5531

Arroyo Grande # 117
955 Rancho Parkway
Arroyo Grande, CA 93420
Phone: 805-474-6114

Bakersfield # 014
8200-C 21 Stockdale Hwy.
Bakersfield, CA 93311
Phone: 661-837-8863

Berkeley #186
1885 University Ave.
Berkeley, CA 94703
Phone: 510-204-9074

Bixby Knolls # 116
4121 Atlantic Ave.
Bixby Knolls, CA 90807
Phone: 562-988-0695

Brea # 011
2500 E. Imperial Hwy. Suite 177
Brea, CA 92821
Phone 714-257-1180

Brentwood # 201
5451 Lone Tree Way
Brentwood, CA 94513
Phone: 925-516-3044

Burbank # 124
214 East Alameda
Burbank, CA 91502
Phone: 818-848-4299

Camarillo # 114
363 Carmen Drive
Camarillo, CA 93010
Phone: 805-388-1925

Campbell # 073
1875 Bascom Avenue
Campbell, CA 95008
Phone: 408-369-7823

Capitola # 064
3555 Clares Street #D
Capitola, CA 95010
Phone: 831-464-0115

Carlsbad # 220
2629 Gateway Road
Carlsbad, CA 92009
Phone: 760-603-8473

Castro Valley # 084
22224 Redwood Road
Castro Valley, CA 94546
Phone: 510-538-2738

Cathedral City # 118
67-720 East Palm Cyn.
Cathedral City, CA 92234
Phone: 760-202-0090

Cerritos # 104
12861 Towne Center Drive
Cerritos, CA 90703
Phone: 562-402-5148

Chatsworth # 184
10330 Mason Ave.
Chatsworth, CA 91311
Phone: 818-341-3010

Chico # 199
801 East Ave., Suite #110
Chico, CA 95926
Phone: 530-343-9920

Chino Hills # 216
13911 Peyton Dr.
Chino Hills, CA 91709
Phone: 909-627-1404

Chula Vista # 120
878 Eastlake Parkway,
Suite 810
Chula Vista, CA 91914
Phone: 619-656-5370

Claremont # 214
475 W. Foothill Blvd.
Claremont, CA 91711
Phone: 909-625-8784

Clovis # 180
1077 N. Willow, Suite 101
Clovis, CA 93611
Phone: 559-325-3120

**Concord (Oak Grove
& Treat) # 083**
785 Oak Grove Road
Concord, CA 94518
Phone: 925-521-1134

Concord (Airport) # 060
1150 Concord Ave.
Concord, CA 94520
Phone: 925-689-2990

Corona # 213
2790 Cabot Drive, Ste. 165
Corona, CA 92883
Phone: 951-603-0299

Costa Mesa # 035
640 W. 17th Street
Costa Mesa, CA 92627
Phone: 949-642-5134

Culver City # 036
9290 Culver Blvd.
Culver City, CA 90232
Phone: 310-202-1108

Daly City # 074
417 Westlake Center
Daly City, CA 94015
Phone: 650-755-3825

Danville # 065
85 Railroad Ave.
Danville, CA 94526
Phone: 925-838-5757

Davis
885 Russell Blvd.
Davis, CA 95616
Phone: 530-757-2693

Eagle Rock # 055
1566 Colorado Blvd.
Eagle Rock, CA 90041
Phone: 323-257-6422

El Cerrito # 108
225 El Cerrito Plaza
El Cerrito, CA 94530
Phone: 510-524-7609

Elk Grove # 190
9670 Bruceville Road
Elk Grove, CA 95757
Phone: 916-686-9980

Emeryville # 072
5700 Christie Avenue
Emeryville, CA 94608
Phone: 510-658-8091

Encinitas # 025
115 N. El Camino Real,
Suite A
Encinitas, CA 92024
Phone: 760-634-2114

Encino # 056
17640 Burbank Blvd.
Encino, CA 91316
Phone: 818-990-7751

Escondido # 105
1885 So. Centre City
Pkwy., Unit "A"
Escondido, CA 92025
Phone: 760-233-4020

Fair Oaks # 071
5309 Sunrise Blvd.
Fair Oaks, CA 95628
Phone: 916-863-1744

Fairfield # 101
1350 Gateway Blvd.,
Suite A1-A7
Fairfield, CA 94533
Phone: 707-434-0144

Folsom # 172
850 East Bidwell
Folsom, CA 95630
Phone: 916-817-8820

Fremont # 077
39324 Argonaut Way
Fremont, CA 94538
Phone: 510-794-1386

Fresno # 008
5376 N. Blackstone
Fresno, CA 93710
Phone: 559-222-4348

Glendale # 053
130 N. Glendale Ave.
Glendale, CA 91206
Phone: 818-637-2990

Goleta # 110
5767 Calle Real
Goleta, CA 93117
Phone: 805-692-2234

Granada Hills # 044
11114 Balboa Blvd.
Granada Hills, CA 91344
Phone: 818-368-6461

Hollywood
1600 N. Vine Street
Los Angeles, CA 90028
Phone: 323-856-0689

Huntington Bch. # 047
18681-101 Main Street
Huntington Bch., CA 92648
Phone: 714-848-9640

Huntington Bch. # 241
21431 Brookhurst St.
Huntington Bch., CA 92646
Phone: 714-968-4070

Huntington Harbor # 244
Huntington Harbour Mall
16821 Algonquin St.
Huntington Bch., CA 92649
Phone: 714-846-7307

Irvine (Walnut Village Center) # 037
14443 Culver Drive
Irvine, CA 92604
Phone: 949-857-8108

Irvine (University Center) # 111
4225 Campus Dr.
Irvine, CA 92612
Phone: 949-509-6138

Irvine (Irvine & Sand Cyn) # 210
6222 Irvine Blvd.
Irvine, CA 92620
Phone: 949-551-6402

La Cañada # 042
475 Foothill Blvd.
La Canada, CA 91011
Phone: 818-790-6373

La Quinta # 189
46-400 Washington Street
La Quinta, CA 92253
Phone: 760-777-1553

Lafayette # 115
3649 Mt. Diablo Blvd.
Lafayette, CA 94549
Phone: 925-299-9344

Laguna Hills # 039
24321 Avenue De La Carlota
Laguna Hills, CA 92653
Phone: 949-586-8453

Laguna Niguel # 103
32351 Street of the Golden
Lantern
Laguna Niguel, CA 92677
Phone: 949-493-8599

La Jolla # 020
8657 Villa LaJolla
Drive #210
La Jolla, CA 92037
Phone: 858-546-8629

La Mesa # 024
5495 Grossmont Center Dr.
La Mesa, CA 91942
Phone: 619-466-0105

Larkspur # 235
2052 Redwood Hwy
Larkspur, CA 94921
Phone: 415-945-7955

Livermore # 208
1122-A East Stanley Blvd.
Livermore, CA 94550
Phone: 925-243-1947

Long Beach (PCH) # 043
6451 E. Pacific Coast Hwy.
Long Beach, CA 90803
Phone: 562-596-4388

Long Beach (Bellflower Blvd.) # 194
2222 Bellflower Blvd.
Long Beach, CA 90815
Phone: 562-596-2514

Los Altos # 127
2310 Homestead Rd.
Los Altos, CA 94024
Phone: 408-245-1917

Los Angeles (Silver Lake) # 017
2738 Hyperion Ave.
Los Angeles, CA 90027
Phone: 323-665-6774

Los Angeles # 031
263 S. La Brea
Los Angeles, CA 90036
Phone: 323-965-1989

Los Angeles (Sunset Strip) # 192
8000 Sunset Blvd.
Los Angeles, CA 90046
Phone: 323-822-7663

Los Gatos # 181
15466 Los Gatos Blvd.
Los Gatos, CA 95032
Phone 408-356-2324

Los Angeles (3rd & Fairfax)
W 3rd St. & S Fairfax Ave
Los Angeles, CA 90048
Phone: 323-931-4012

Manhattan Beach # 034
1821 Manhattan
Beach. Blvd.
Manhattan Bch., CA 90266
Phone: 310-372-1274

Manhattan Beach # 196
1800 Rosecrans Blvd.
Manhattan Beach,
CA 90266
Phone: 310-725-9800

Menlo Park # 069
720 Menlo Avenue
Menlo Park, CA 94025
Phone: 650-323-2134

Millbrae # 170
765 Broadway
Millbrae, CA 94030
Phone: 650-259-9142

Mission Viejo # 126
25410 Marguerite Parkway
Mission Viejo, CA 92692
Phone: 949-581-5638

Modesto # 009
3250 Dale Road
Modesto, CA 95356
Phone: 209-491-0445

Monrovia # 112
604 W. Huntington Dr.
Monrovia, CA 91016
Phone: 626-358-8884

Monterey # 204
570 Munras Ave., Ste. 20
Monterey, CA 93940
Phone: 831-372-2010

Montrose
2462 Honolulu Ave.
Montrose, CA 91020
Phone: 818-957-3613

Morgan Hill # 202
17035 Laurel Road
Morgan Hill, CA 95037
Phone: 408-778-6409

Mountain View # 081
590 Showers Dr.
Mountain View, CA 94040
Phone: 650-917-1013

Napa # 128
3654 Bel Aire Plaza
Napa, CA 94558
Phone: 707-256-0806

Newbury Park # 243
125 N. Reino Road
Newbury Park, CA
Phone: 805-375-1984

Newport Beach # 125
8086 East Coast Highway
Newport Beach, CA 92657
Phone: 949-494-7404

Novato # 198
7514 Redwood Blvd.
Novato, CA 94945
Phone: 415-898-9359

Oakland (Lakeshore) # 203
3250 Lakeshore Ave.
Oakland, CA 94610
Phone: 510-238-9076

Oakland (Rockridge) # 231
5727 College Ave.
Oakland, CA 94618
Phone: 510-923-9428

Oceanside # 22
2570 Vista Way
Oceanside, CA 92054
Phone: 760-433-9994

Orange # 046
2114 N. Tustin St.
Orange, CA 92865
Phone: 714-283-5697

Pacific Grove # 008
1170 Forest Avenue
Pacific Grove, CA 93950
Phone: 831-656-0180

Palm Desert # 003
44-250 Town Center Way,
Suite C6
Palm Desert, CA 92260
Phone: 760-340-2291

Palmdale # 185
39507 10th Street West
Palmdale, CA 93551
Phone: 661-947-2890

Palo Alto # 207
855 El Camino Real
Palo Alto, CA 94301
Phone: 650-327-7018

Pasadena (S. Lake Ave.) # 179
345 South Lake Ave.
Pasadena, CA 91101
Phone: 626-395-9553

Pasadena (S. Arroyo Pkwy.) # 051
610 S. Arroyo Parkway
Pasadena, CA 91105
Phone: 626-568-9254

Pasadena (Hastings Ranch) # 171
467 Rosemead Blvd.
Pasadena, CA 91107
Phone: 626-351-3399

Petaluma # 107
169 North McDowell Blvd.
Petaluma, CA 94954
Phone: 707-769-2782

Pinole # 230
2742 Pinole Valley Rd.
Pinole, CA 94564
Phone: 510-222-3501

Pleasanton # 066
4040 Pimlico #150
Pleasanton, CA 94588
Phone: 925-225-3600

Rancho Cucamonga # 217
6401 Haven Ave.
Rancho Cucamonga,
CA 91737
Phone: 909-476-1410

Rancho Palos Verdes # 057
28901 S. Western Ave. #243
Rancho Palos Verdes,
CA 90275
Phone: 310-832-1241

Rancho Palos Verdes # 233
31176 Hawthorne Blvd.
Rancho Palos Verdes, CA
90275
Phone: 310-544-1727

Rancho Santa Margarita # 027
30652 Santa Margarita Pkwy.
Suite F102
Rancho Santa Margarita,
CA 92688
Phone: 949-888-3640

Redding # 219
845 Browning St.
Redding, CA 96003
Phone: 530-223-4875

Redlands # 099
552 Orange Street Plaza
Redlands, CA 92374
Phone: 909-798-3888

Redondo Beach # 038
1761 S. Elena Avenue
Redondo Bch., CA 90277
Phone: 310-316-1745

Riverside # 15
6225 Riverside Plaza
Riverside, CA 92506
Phone: 951-682-4684

Roseville # 80
1117 Roseville Square
Roseville, CA 95678
Phone: 916-784-9084

Sacramento (Folsom Blvd.) # 175
5000 Folsom Blvd.
Sacramento, CA 95819
Phone: 916-456-1853

Sacramento (Fulton & Marconi) # 070
2625 Marconi Avenue
Sacramento, CA 95821
Phone: 916-481-8797

San Carlos # 174
1482 El Camino Real
San Carlos, CA 94070
Phone: 650-594-2138

San Clemente # 016
638 Camino DeLosMares,
Sp.#115-G
San Clemente, CA 92673
Phone: 949-240-9996

San Diego (Hillcrest) # 026
1090 University Ste.
G100-107
San Diego, CA 92103
Phone: 619-296-3122

San Diego (Point Loma) # 188
2401 Truxtun Rd., Ste. 300
San Diego, CA 92106
Phone: 619-758-9272

San Diego (Pacific Beach) # 021
1211 Garnet Avenue
San Diego, CA 92109
Phone: 858-272-7235

San Diego (Carmel Mtn. Ranch) # 023
11955 Carmel Mtn. Rd. #702
San Diego, CA 92128
Phone: 858-673-0526

San Diego (Scripps Ranch) # 221
9850 Hibert Street
San Diego, CA 92131
Phone: 858-549-9185

San Dimas # 028
856 Arrow Hwy. "C"
Target Center
San Dimas, CA 91773
Phone: 909-305-4757

San Francisco (9th Street) # 078
555 9th Street
San Francisco, CA 94103
Phone: 415-863-1292

San Francisco (Masonic Ave.) # 100
3 Masonic Avenue
San Francisco, CA 94118
Phone: 415-346-9964

San Francisco (Nob Hill)
1095 Hyde St.
San Francisco, CA 94109
Phone: 415-292-7665

San Francisco (North Beach) #019
410 Bay Street
San Francisco, CA 94133
Phone: 415-351-1013

San Francisco (Stonestown) # 236
265 Winston Dr.
San Francisco, CA 94132
Phone: 415-665-1835

San Gabriel # 032
7260 N. Rosemead Blvd.
San Gabriel, CA 91775
Phone: 626-285-5862

San Jose (Bollinger) # 232
7250 Bollinger Rd.
San Jose, CA 95129
Phone: 408-873-7384

San Jose (Coleman Ave) # 212
635 Coleman Ave.
San Jose, CA 95110
Phone: 408-298-9731

San Jose (Old Almaden) # 063
5353 Almaden Expressway
#J-38
San Jose, CA 95118
Phone: 408-927-9091

San Jose (Westgate West) # 062
5269 Prospect
San Jose, CA 95129
Phone: 408-446-5055

San Luis Obispo # 041
3977 Higuera Street
San Luis Obispo, CA 93401
Phone: 805-783-2780

San Mateo (Grant Street) # 067
1820-22 S. Grant Street
San Mateo, CA 94402
Phone: 650-570-6140

San Mateo (Hillsdale) # 245
45 W Hillsdale Blvd
San Mateo, CA 94403
Phone: 650-286-1509

San Rafael # 061
337 Third Street
San Rafael, CA 94901
Phone: 415-454-9530

Santa Ana # 113
3329 South Bristol Street
Santa Ana, CA 92704
Phone: 714-424-9304

Santa Barbara (S. Milpas St.) # 059
29 S. Milpas Street
Santa Barbara, CA 93103
Phone: 805-564-7878

Santa Barbara (De La Vina) # 183
3025 De La Vina
Santa Barbara, CA 93105
Phone: 805-563-7383

Santa Cruz # 193
700 Front Street
Santa Cruz, CA 95060
Phone: 831-425-0140

Santa Maria # 239
1303 S. Bradley Road
Santa Maria, CA 93454
Phone: 805-925-1657

Santa Monica # 006
3212 Pico Blvd.
Santa Monica, CA 90405
Phone: 310-581-0253

**Santa Rosa
(Cleveland Ave.) # 075**
3225 Cleveland Avenue
Santa Rosa, CA 95403
Phone: 707-525-1406

**Santa Rosa
(Santa Rosa Ave.) # 178**
2100 Santa Rosa Ave.
Santa Rosa, CA 95407
Phone: 707-535-0788

Sherman Oaks # 049
14119 Riverside Drive
Sherman Oaks, CA 91423
Phone: 818-789-2771

Simi Valley # 030
2975-A Cochran St.
Simi Valley, CA 93065
Phone: 805-520-3135

South Pasadena # 018
613 Mission Street
South Pasadena, CA 91030
Phone: 626-441-6263

South San Francisco # 187
301 McLellan Dr.
So. San Francisco,
CA 94080
Phone: 650-583-6401

Stockton # 076
6535 Pacific Avenue
Stockton, CA 95207
Phone: 209-951-7597

Studio City # 122
11976 Ventura Blvd.
Studio City, CA 91604
Phone: 818-509-0168

Sunnyvale # 068
727 Sunnyvale/
Saratoga Rd.
Sunnyvale, CA 94087
Phone: 408-481-9082

Temecula # 102
40665 Winchester Rd.,
Bldg. B, Ste. 4-6
Temecula, CA 92591
Phone: 951-296-9964

Templeton # 211
1111 Rossi Road
Templeton, CA 93465
Phone: 805-434-9562

Thousand Oaks # 196
451 Avenida
De Los Arboles
Thousand Oaks, CA 91360
Phone: 805-492-7107

Toluca Lake # 054
10130 Riverside Drive
Toluca Lake, CA 91602
Phone: 818-762-2787

**Torrance
(Hawthorne Blvd.) # 121**
19720 Hawthorne Blvd.
Torrance, CA 90503
Phone: 310-793-8585

**Torrance (Rolling
Hills Plaza) # 029**
2545 Pacific Coast Highway
Torrance, CA 90505
Phone: 310-326-9520

Tustin # 197
12932 Newport Avenue
Tustin, CA 92780
Phone: 714-669-3752

Upland # 010
333 So. Mountain Avenue
Upland, CA 91786
Phone: 909-946-4799

Valencia # 013
26517 Bouquet Canyon Rd
Santa Clarita, CA 91350
Phone: 661-263-3796

Ventura # 045
1795 S. Victoria Avenue
Ventura, CA 93003
Phone: 805-650-9977

Ventura – Midtown
103 S. Mills Road Suite 104
Ventura, CA 93003
Phone: 805-658-2664

Walnut Creek # 123
1372 So. California Blvd.
Walnut Creek, CA 94596
Phone: 925-945-1674

West Hills # 050
6751 Fallbrook Ave.
West Hills, CA 91307
Phone: 818-347-2591

West Hollywood # 040
7304 Santa Monica Blvd.
West Hollywood, CA 90046
Phone: 323-851-9772

West Hollywood # 173
8611 Santa Monica Blvd.
West Hollywood, CA 90069
Phone: 310-657-0152

**West Los Angeles
(National Blvd.) # 007**
10850 National Blvd.
West Los Angeles, CA 90064
Phone: 310-470-1917

**West Los Angeles
S. Sepulveda Blvd.) # 119**
3456 S. Sepulveda Blvd.
West Los Angeles, CA 90034
Phone: 310-836-2458

**West Los Angeles
(Olympic) # 215**
11755 W. Olympic Blvd.
West Los Angeles,
CA 90064
Phone: 310-477-5949

Westchester # 033
8645 S. Sepulveda
Westchester, CA 90045
Phone: 310-338-9238

Westlake Village # 058
3835 E. Thousand
Oaks Blvd.
Westlake Village, CA 91362
Phone: 805-494-5040

Westwood # 234
1000 Glendon Avenue
Los Angeles, CA 90024
Phone: 310-824-1495

Whittier # 048
15025 E. Whittier Blvd.
Whittier, CA 90603
Phone: 562-698-1642

Woodland Hills # 209
21054 Clarendon St.
Woodland Hills, CA 91364
Phone: 818-712-9475

Yorba Linda # 176
19655 Yorba Linda Blvd.
Yorba Linda, CA 92886
Phone: 714-970-0116

Connecticut

Danbury # 525
113 Mill Plain Rd.
Danbury, CT 06811
Phone: 203-739-0098
Alcohol: Beer Only

Darien # 522
436 Boston Post Rd.
Darien, CT 06820
Phone: 203-656-1414
Alcohol: Beer Only

Fairfield # 523
2258 Black Rock Turnpike
Fairfield, CT 06825
Phone: 203-330-8301
Alcohol: Beer Only

Orange # 524
560 Boston Post Road
Orange, CT 06477
Phone: 203-795-5505
Alcohol: Beer Only

West Hartford # 526
1489 New Britain Ave.
West Hartford, CT 06110
Phone: 860-561-4771
Alcohol: Beer Only

Westport # 521
400 Post Road East
Westport, CT 06880
Phone: 203-226-8966
Alcohol: Beer Only

Delaware

Wilmington* # 536
5605 Concord Pike
Wilmington, DE 19803
Phone: 302-478-8494

District of Columbia

Washington # 653
1101 25th Street NW
Washington, DC 20037
Phone: 202-296-1921

Florida

Gainesville – Coming Soon!
3724 SW Archer Rd.
Gainesville, GL 32608
Phone: TBD

Naples
10600 Tamiami Trail North
Naples, FL 34108
Phone: 239-596-5631

Sarasota
4101 S. Tamiami Trail
Sarasota, FL 34231
Phone: 941-922-5727

Georgia

Athens
1850 Epps Bridge Parkway
Athens, GA 30606
Phone: 706-583-8934

**Atlanta
(Buckhead) # 735**
3183 Peachtree Rd NE
Atlanta, GA 30305
Phone: 404-842-0907

Atlanta (Midtown) # 730
931 Monroe Dr., NE
Atlanta, GA 30308
Phone: 404-815-9210

Marietta # 732
4250 Roswell Road
Marietta, GA 30062
Phone: 678-560-3585

Norcross # 734
5185 Peachtree Parkway,
Bld. 1200
Norcross, GA 30092
Phone: 678-966-9236

Roswell # 733
635 W. Crossville Road
Roswell, GA 30075
Phone: 770-645-8505

Sandy Springs # 731
6277 Roswell Road NE
Sandy Springs, GA 30328
Phone: 404-236-2414

Illinois

Algonquin # 699
1800 South Randall Road
Algonquin, IL 60102
Phone: 847-854-4886

Arlington Heights # 687
17 W. Rand Road
Arlington Heights, IL 60004
Phone: 847-506-0752

Batavia # 689
1942 West Fabyan
Parkway #222
Batavia, IL 60510
Phone: 630-879-3234

Chicago (Diversey Pkwy)
667 W. Diversey Pkwy
Chicago, IL 60614
Phone: 773-935-7255

**Chicago
(Lincoln & Grace) # 688**
3745 North Lincoln Avenue
Chicago, IL 60613
Phone: 773-248-4920

**Chicago
(Lincoln Park) # 691**
1840 North Clybourn
Avenue #200
Chicago, IL 60614
Phone: 312-274-9733

**Chicago
(River North) # 696**
44 E. Ontario St.
Chicago, IL 60611
Phone: 312-951-6369

Chicago (South Loop)
1147 S. Wabash Ave.
Chicago, IL 60605
Phone: 312-588-0489

Downers Grove # 683
122 Ogden Ave.
Downers Grove, IL 60515
Phone: 630-241-1662

Glen Ellyn # 680
680 Roosevelt Rd.
Glen Ellyn, IL 60137
Phone: 630-858-5077

Glenview # 681
1407 Waukegan Road
Glenview, IL 60025
Phone: 847-657-7821

La Grange # 685
25 North La Grange Road
La Grange, IL 60525
Phone: 708-579-0838

Lake Zurich # 684
735 W. Route 22**
Lake Zurich, IL 60047
Phone: 847-550-7827
[**For accurate driving
directions using
GPS, please use
735 W Main Street]

Naperville # 690
44 West Gartner Road
Naperville, IL 60540
Phone: 630-355-4389

Northbrook # 682
127 Skokie Blvd.
Northbrook, IL 60062
Phone: 847-498-9076

Oak Park # 697
483 N. Harlem Ave.
Oak Park, IL 60301
Phone: 708-386-1169

Orland Park # 686
14924 S. La Grange Road
Orland Park, IL 60462
Phone: 708-349-9021

Park Ridge # 698
190 North Northwest Hwy
Park Ridge, IL 60068
Phone: 847-292-1108

Indiana

**Indianapolis
(Castleton) # 671**
5473 East 82nd Street
Indianapolis, IN 46250
Phone: 317-595-8950

**Indianapolis
(West 86th) # 670**
2902 West 86th Street
Indianapolis, IN 46268
Phone: 317-337-1880

Iowa

West Des Moines
6305 Mills Civic Parkway
West Des Moines, IA 50266
Phone: 515-225-3820

Kansas

Leawood* #723
4201 W 119th Street
Leawood, KS 66209
Phone: 913-327-7209

Kentucky

Louisville
4600 Shelbyville Road
Louisville, KY 40207
Phone: 502-895-1361

Lexington Grocery
2326 Nicholasville Rd
Lexington, KY 40503
Phone: 859-313-5030

Lexington Wine
2320 Nicholasville Rd
Lexington, KY 40503
Phone: 859-277-0144

Maine

Portland # 519
87 Marginal Way
Portland, ME 04101
Phone: 207-699-3799

Maryland

Annapolis* # 650
160 F Jennifer Road
Annapolis, MD 21401
Phone: 410-573-0505

Bethesda* # 645
6831 Wisconsin Avenue
Bethesda, MD 20815
Phone: 301-907-0982

Columbia* # 658
6610 Marie Curie Dr.
(Int. of 175 & 108)
Elkridge, MD 21075
Phone: 410-953-8139

Gaithersburg* # 648
18270 Contour Rd.
Gaithersburg, MD 20877
Phone: 301-947-5953

Pikesville* # 655
1809 Reisterstown Road,
Suite #121
Pikesville, MD 21208
Phone: 410-484-8373

Rockville* # 642
12268-H Rockville Pike
Rockville, MD 20852
Phone: 301-468-6656

Silver Spring* # 652
10741 Columbia Pike
Silver Spring, MD 20901
Phone: 301-681-1675

Towson* # 649
1 E. Joppa Rd.
Towson, MD 21286
Phone: 410-296-9851

Massachusetts

Acton* # 511
145 Great Road
Acton, MA 01720
Phone: 978-266-8908

Arlington* # 505
1427 Massachusetts Ave.
Arlington, MA 02476
Phone: 781-646-9138

Boston #510
899 Boylston Street
Boston, MA 02115
Phone: 617-262-6505

Brookline # 501
1317 Beacon Street
Brookline, MA 02446
Phone: 617-278-9997

Burlington* # 515
51 Middlesex Turnpike
Burlington, MA 01803
Phone: 781-273-2310

Cambridge
748 Memorial Drive
Cambridge, MA 02139
Phone: 617-491-8582

**Cambridge
(Fresh Pond)* # 517**
211 Alewife Brook Pkwy
Cambridge, MA 02138
Phone: 617-498-3201

Framingham # 503
659 Worcester Road
Framingham, MA 01701
Phone: 508-935-2931

Hadley* # 512
375 Russell Street
Hadley, MA 01035
Phone: 413-587-3260

Hanover* # 513
1775 Washington Street
Hanover, MA 02339
Phone: 781-826-5389

Hyannis* # 514
Christmas Tree Promenade
655 Route 132, Unit 4-A
Hyannis, MA 02601
Phone: 508-790-3008

Needham Hts* 504
958 Highland Avenue
Needham Hts, MA 02494
Phone: 781-449-6993

Peabody* # 516
300 Andover Street,
Suite 15
Peabody, MA 01960
Phone: 978-977-5316

Saugus* # 506
358 Broadway, Unit B
(Shops @ Saugus, Rte. 1)
Saugus, MA 01906
Phone: 781-231-0369

Shrewsbury* # 508
77 Boston Turnpike
Shrewsbury, MA 01545
Phone: 508-755-9560

West Newton* # 509
1121 Washington St.
West Newton, MA 02465
Phone: 617-244-1620

Michigan

Ann Arbor # 678
2398 East Stadium Blvd.
Ann Arbor, MI 48104
Phone: 734-975-2455

Farmington Hills # 675
31221 West 14 Mile Road
Farmington Hills, MI 48334
Phone: 248-737-4609

Grosse Pointe # 665
17028 Kercheval Ave.
Grosse Pointe, MI 48230
Phone: 313-640-7794

Northville # 667
20490 Haggerty Road
Northville, MI 48167
Phone: 734-464-3675

Rochester Hills # 668
3044 Walton Blvd.
Rochester Hills, MI 48309
Phone: 248-375-2190

Royal Oak # 674
27880 Woodward Ave.
Royal Oak, MI 48067
Phone: 248-582-9002

Minnesota

Bloomington
4270 W. 78th St.
Bloomington, MN 55435
Phone: 952-835-8640

Maple Grove # 713
12105 Elm Creek Blvd. N.
Maple Grove, MN 55369
Phone: 763-315-1739

Minnetonka # 714
11220 Wayzata Blvd
Minnetonka, MN 55305
Phone: 952-417-9080

Rochester
1200 16th St. SW
Rochester, NY 55902
Phone: 952-417-9080

St. Louis Park # 710
4500 Excelsior Blvd.
St. Louis Park, MN 55416
Phone: 952-285-1053

St. Paul # 716
484 Lexington Parkway S.
St. Paul, MN 55116
Phone: 651-698-3119

Woodbury # 715
8960 Hudson Road
Woodbury, MN 55125
Phone: 651-735-0269

Missouri

Brentwood # 792
48 Brentwood
Promenade Court
Brentwood, MO 63144
Phone: 314-963-0253

Chesterfield # 693
1679 Clarkson Road
Chesterfield, MO 63017
Phone: 636-536-7846

Creve Coeur # 694
11505 Olive Blvd.
Creve Coeur, MO 63141
Phone: 314-569-0427

Des Peres # 695
13343 Manchester Rd.
Des Peres, MO 63131
Phone: 314-984-5051

Kansas City
8600 Ward Parkway
Kansas City, MO 64114
Phone: 816-333-5322

Nebraska

Lincoln
3120 Pine Lake Road, Suite R
Lincoln, NE 68516
Phone: 402-328-0120

Omaha # 714
10305 Pacific St.
Omaha, NE 68114
Phone: 402-391-3698

Nevada

Anthem # 280
10345 South Eastern Ave.
Henderson, NV 89052
Phone: 702-407-8673

Carson City # 281
3790 US Highway 395 S,
Suite 401
Carson City, NV 89705
Phone: 775-267-2486

Henderson # 097
2716 North Green Valley
Parkway
Henderson, NV 89014
Phone: 702-433-6773

**Las Vegas
(Decatur Blvd.) # 098**
2101 S. Decatur Blvd., Suite 25
Las Vegas, NV 89102
Phone: 702-367-0227

Las Vegas (Summerlin) # 086
7575 West Washington,
Suite 117
Las Vegas, NV 89128
Phone: 702-242-8240

Reno # 082
5035 S. McCarran Blvd.
Reno, NV 89502
Phone: 775-826-1621

New Hampshire

Nashua – Coming Soon!
262 Daniel Webster Hwy
Nashua, NH 03060
Phone: TBD

*Newington (Portsmouth) –
Coming Soon!*
45 Gosling Rd
Newington, NH 03801
Phone: TBD

New Jersey

Edgewater* # 606
715 River Road
Edgewater, NJ 07020
Phone: 201-945-5932

Florham Park* # 604
186 Columbia Turnpike
Florham Park, NJ 07932
Phone: 973-514-1511

Marlton* # 631
300 P Route 73 South
Marlton, NJ 08053
Phone: 856-988-3323

Millburn* # 609
187 Millburn Ave.
Millburn, NJ 07041
Phone: 973-218-0912

Paramus* # 605
404 Rt. 17 North
Paramus, NJ 07652
Phone: 201-265-9624

Princeton # 607
3528 US 1
(Brunswick Pike)
Princeton, NJ 08540
Phone: 609-897-0581

Shrewsbury*
1031 Broad St.
Shrewsbury, NJ 07702
Phone: 732-389-2535

Wayne* # 632
1172 Hamburg Turnpike
Wayne, NJ 07470
Phone: 973-692-0050

Westfield # 601
155 Elm St.
Westfield, NJ 07090
Phone: 908-301-0910

Westwood* # 602
20 Irvington Street
Westwood, NJ 07675
Phone: 201-263-0134

New Mexico

Albuquerque # 166
8928 Holly Ave. NE
Albuquerque, NM 87122
Phone: 505-796-0311

**Albuquerque
(Uptown) # 167**
2200 Uptown Loop NE
Albuquerque, NM 87110
Phone: 505-883-3662

Santa Fe # 165
530 W. Cordova Road
Santa Fe, NM 87505
Phone: 505-995-8145

New York

NY stores sell beer only

Brooklyn # 558
130 Court St
Brooklyn, NY 11201
Phone: 718-246-8460

Colonie (Albany)
79 Wolf Road
Colonie, NY 12205
Phone: 51-482-4538

Commack # 551
5010 Jericho Turnpike
Commack, NY 11725
Phone: 631-493-9210

Hartsdale # 533
215 North Central Avenue
Hartsdale, NY 10530
Phone: 914-997-1960

Hewlett # 554
1280 West Broadway
Hewlett, NY 11557
Phone: 516-569-7191

Lake Grove # 556
137 Alexander Ave.
Lake Grove, NY 11755
Phone: 631-863-2477

Larchmont # 532
1260 Boston Post Road
Larchmont, NY 10538
Phone: 914-833-9110

Merrick # 553
1714 Merrick Road
Merrick, NY 11566
Phone: 516-771-1012

**New York
(72nd & Broadway) # 542**
2075 Broadway
New York, NY 10023
Phone: 212-799-0028

**New York
(Chelsea) # 543**
675 6th Ave
New York, NY 10010
Phone: 212-255-2106

**New York (Union Square
Grocery) # 540**
142 E. 14th St.
New York, NY 10003
Phone: 212-529-4612

**New York (Union Square
Wine) # 541**
138 E. 14th St.
New York, NY 10003
Phone: 212-529-6326
Alcohol: Wine Only

Oceanside # 552
3418 Long Beach Rd.
Oceanside, NY 11572
Phone: 516-536-9163

Plainview # 555
425 S. Oyster Bay Rd.
Plainview, NY 11803
Phone: 516-933-6900

Queens # 557
90-30 Metropolitan Ave.
Queens, NY 11374
Phone: 718-275-1791

Rochester
3349 Monroe Ave
Rochester, NY 14618
Phone: 585-248-5011

Scarsdale # 531
727 White Plains Rd.
Scarsdale, NY 10583
Phone: 914-472-2988

Staten Island
2385 Richmond Ave
Staten Island, NY 10314
Phone: 718-370-1085

Westbury
900 Old Country Road
Garden City, NY 11530
Phone: Phone# 516-794-0174

North Carolina

Cary # 741
1393 Kildaire Farms Rd.
Cary, NC 27511
Phone: 919-465-5984

Chapel Hill # 745
1800 E. Franklin St.
Chapel Hill, NC 27514
Phone: 919-918-7871

**Charlotte
(Midtown) # 744**
1133 Metropolitan Ave.,
Ste. 100
Charlotte, NC 28204
Phone: 704-334-0737

Charlotte (North) # 743
1820 East Arbors Dr.**
(corner of W. Mallard Creek
Church Rd. & Senator
Royall Dr.)
Charlotte, NC 28262
Phone: 704-688-9578
[**For accurate driving
directions on the web, please
use 1820 W. Mallard Creek
Church Rd.]

Charlotte (South) # 742
6418 Rea Rd.
Charlotte, NC 28277
Phone: 704-543-5249

Raleigh # 746
3000 Wake Forest Rd.
Raleigh, NC 27609
Phone: 919-981-7422

Wilmington
1437 S. College Road
Wilmington, NC 28403
Phone: 919-981-7422

Winston-Salem
252 S. Stratford Road
Winston Salem, NC 27103
Phone: 336-721-1744

Ohio

Cincinnati # 669
7788 Montgomery Road
Cincinnati, OH 45236
Phone: 513-984-3452

Columbus # 679
3888 Townsfair Way
Columbus, OH 43219
Phone: 614-473-0794

Dublin # 672
6355 Sawmill Road
Dublin, OH 43017
Phone: 614-793-8505

Kettering # 673
328 East Stroop Road
Kettering, OH 45429
Phone: 937-294-5411

Westlake # 677
175 Market Street
Westlake, OH 44145
Phone: 440-250-1592

Woodmere # 676
28809 Chagrin Blvd.
Woodmere, OH 44122
Phone: 216-360-9320

Oregon

Beaverton # 141
11753 S. W. Beaverton
Hillsdale Hwy.
Beaverton, OR 97005
Phone: 503-626-3794

Bend # 150
63455 North
Highway 97, Ste. 4
Bend, OR 97701
Phone: 541-312-4198

Clackamas # 152
9345 SE 82nd Ave (across
from Home Depot)
Happy Valley, OR 97086
Phone: 503-771-6300

Corvallis # 154
1550 NW 9th Street
Corvallis, OR 97330
Phone: 541-753-0048

Eugene # 145
85 Oakway Center
Eugene, OR 97401
Phone: 541-485-1744

Hillsboro # 149
2285 NW 185th Ave.
Hillsboro, OR 97124
Phone: 503-645-8321

Lake Oswego # 142
15391 S. W. Bangy Rd.
Lake Oswego, OR 97035
Phone: 503-639-3238

Medford
Northgate Marketplace
1500 Court St.
Medford, OR 97501
Phone: 541-608-4993

Portland (SE) # 143
4715 S. E. 39th Avenue
Portland, OR 97202
Phone: 503-777-1601

Portland (NW) # 146
2122 N.W. Glisan
Portland, OR 97210
Phone: 971-544-0788

**Portland
(Hollywood) # 144**
4121 N.E. Halsey St.
Portland, OR 97213
Phone: 503-284-1694

Salem #153
4450 Commercial St.,
Suite 100
Salem, OR 97302
Phone: 503-378-9042

Pennsylvania

Ardmore* # 635
112 Coulter Avenue
Ardmore, PA 19003
Phone: 610-658-0645

Jenkintown* # 633
933 Old York Road
Jenkintown, PA 19046
Phone: 215-885-524

Media* # 637
12 East State Street
Media, PA 19063
Phone: 610-891-2752

North Wales* # 639
1430 Bethlehem Pike
(corner SR 309 & SR 63)
North Wales, PA 19454
Phone: 215-646-5870

Philadelphia* # 634
2121 Market Street
Philadelphia, PA 19103
Phone: 215-569-9282

Pittsburgh* # 638
6343 Penn Ave.
Pittsburgh, PA 15206
Phone: 412-363-5748

Pittsburgh*
1630 Washington Road
Pittsburgh, PA 15228
Phone: 412-835-2212

State College*
1855 North Atherton St.
State College, PA 16803
Phone: 814-234-2224

Wayne* # 632
171 East Swedesford Rd.
Wayne, PA 19087
Phone: 610-225-0925

Rhode Island

Warwick* # 518
1000 Bald Hill Rd
Warwick, RI 02886
Phone: 401-821-5368

South Carolina

Columbia – Coming Soon!
4502 Forest Drive
Columbia, SC 29206
Phone: TBD

Greenville
59 Woodruff
Industrial Lane
Greenville, SC 29607
Phone: 864-286-0231

Mt. Pleasant – #752
401 Johnnie Dodds Blvd.
Mt. Pleasant, SC 29464
Phone: 843-884-4037

Tennessee

Knoxville
8025 Kingston Pike
Knoxville, TN 37919
Phone: 865-670-4088
Alcohol: Beer Only

Nashville # 664
3909 Hillsboro Pike
Nashville, TN 37215
Phone: 615-297-6560
Alcohol: Beer Only

Texas

Austin – Coming Soon!
211 Seaholm Dr, Ste 100
Austin, TX 78703

*Dallas (Lower Greenville) –
Coming Soon!*
2001 Greenville Ave
Dallas, TX 75206

*Dallas (Preston Hallow
Village) – Coming Soon!*
Central Expy & Walnut
Hill Ln

Fort Worth
2701 S. Hulen St
For Worth, TX 76107
Phone: 817-922-9107

Houston (Alabama Theater)
2922 S Shepherd Dr
Houston, TX 77098
Phone: 713-526-4034

*Houston (Memorial Area) –
Coming Soon!*
1440 S Voss Road
Houston, TX 77057

Plano
2400 Preston Rd Ste 200
Plano, TX 75093
Phone: 972-312-9538

San Antonio – Coming Soon!
350 East Basse Rd
San Antonio, TX 78209

The Woodlands
10868 Kuykendahl Road
The Woodlands, TX 77381
Phone: 281-465-0254

Utah

*Salt Lake City – Coming
Soon!*
634 East 400 South
Salt Lake City, UT 84102
Phone: TBD

Virginia

Alexandria # 647
612 N. Saint Asaph Street
Alexandria, VA 22314
Phone: 703-548-0611

Bailey's Crossroads # 644
5847 Leesburg Pike
Bailey's Crossroads,
VA 22041
Phone: 703-379-5883

Centreville # 654
14100 Lee Highway
Centreville, VA 20120
Phone: 703-815-0697

Charlottesville
2025 Bond St.
Charlottesville, VA 22901
Phone: 434-974-1466

Clarendon
1109 N. Highland St.
Arlington, VA 22201
Phone: 703-351-8015

Fairfax # 643
9464 Main Street
Fairfax, VA 22031
Phone: 703-764-8550

Falls Church # 641
7514 Leesburg Turnpike
Falls Church, VA 22043
Phone: 703-288-0566

Newport News # 656
12551 Jefferson Ave.,
Suite #179
Newport News, VA 23602
Phone: 757-890-0235

Reston # 646
11958 Killingsworth Ave.
Reston, VA 20194
Phone: 703-689-0865

**Richmond
(Short Pump) # 659**
11331 W Broad St, Ste 161
Glen Allen, VA 23060
Phone: 804-360-4098

Springfield # 651
6394 Springfield Plaza
Springfield, VA 22150
Phone: 703-569-9301

Virginia Beach # 660
503 Hilltop Plaza
Virginia Beach, VA 23454
Phone: 757-422-4840

Williamsburg # 657
5000 Settlers Market Blvd
(corner of Monticello and
Settlers Market)**
Williamsburg, VA 23188
Phone: 757-259-2135
[**For accurate driving
directions on the web, please
use 5224 Monticello Ave.]

Washington

Ballard # 147
4609 14th Avenue NW
Seattle, WA 98107
Phone: 206-783-0498

Bellevue # 131
15400 N. E. 20th Street
Bellevue, WA 98007
Phone: 425-643-6885

Bellingham # 151
2410 James Street
Bellingham, WA 98225
Phone: 360-734-5166

Burien # 133
15868 1st. Avenue South
Burien, WA 98148
Phone: 206-901-9339

Everett # 139
811 S.E. Everett Mall Way
Everett, WA 98208
Phone: 425-513-2210

Federal Way # 134
1758 S. 320th Street
Federal Way, WA 98003
Phone: 253-529-9242

Issaquah # 138
1495 11th Ave. N.W.
Issaquah, WA 98027
Phone: 425-837-8088

Kirkland # 132
12632 120th Avenue N. E.
Kirkland, WA 98034
Phone: 425-823-1685

Lynnwood # 129
19500 Highway 99,
Suite 100
Lynnwood, WA 98036
Phone: 425-744-1346

Olympia # 156
Olympia West Center
1530 Black Lake Blvd.
Olympia, WA 98502
Phone: 360-352-744

Redmond # 140
15932 Redmond Way
Redmond, WA 98052
Phone: 425-883-1624

Seattle (U. District) # 137
4555 Roosevelt Way NE
Seattle, WA 98105
Phone: 206-547-6299

**Seattle
(Queen Anne Hill) # 135**
112 West Galer St.
Seattle, WA 98119
Phone: 206-378-5536

Seattle (Capitol Hill) # 130
1700 Madison St.
Seattle, WA 98122
Phone: 206-322-7268

Seattle (West)
4545 Fauntleroy Way SW
Seattle, WA 98116
Phone: 206-913-0013
Silverdale
9991 Mickelberry Rd.
Silverdale, WA 98383
Phone: 360-307-7224

Spokane
2975 East 29th Avenue
Spokane, WA 99223
Phone: 509-534-1077

University Place # 148
3800 Bridgeport Way West
University Place, WA 98466
Phone: 253-460-2672

Vancouver # 136
305 SE Chkalov Drive #B1
Vancouver, WA 98683
Phone: 360-883-9000

Wisconsin

Brookfield
12665 W. Bluemound Rd
Brookfield, WI 53005
Phone: 262-784-4806

Glendale # 711
5600 North Port
Washington Road
Glendale, WI 53217
Phone: 414-962-3382

Madison # 712
1810 Monroe Street
Madison, WI 53711
Phone: 608-257-1916

*Although we aim to
ensure that the store
location information
contained here is
correct, we will not
be responsible for any
errors or omissions.*

Photo / Image Credits

Photography of recipes © Deana Gunn and Wona Miniati

Used under license from **shutterstock.com**: *(*many of the images appear on multiple pages)*w

Other titles in this cookbook series:

Cooking with All Things Trader Joe's
by Deana Gunn & Wona Miniati
ISBN 978-0-9799384-8-1

Cooking with Trader Joe's: Companion
by Deana Gunn & Wona Miniati
ISBN 978-0-9799384-9-8

Cooking with Trader Joe's: Dinner's Done!
by Deana Gunn & Wona Miniati
ISBN 978-0-9799384-3-6

Cooking with Trader Joe's: Pack A Lunch!
by Céline Cossou-Bordes
ISBN 978-0-9799384-5-0

Cooking with Trader Joe's: Skinny Dish! (Vegan)
by Jennifer K. Reilly, RD
ISBN 978-0-9799384-7-4

Cooking with Trader Joe's: Lighten Up!
by Susan Greeley, MS, RD
ISBN 978-0-9799384-6-7

Cooking with Trader Joe's: Easy Lunch Boxes
by Kelly Lester
ISBN 978-1-938706-00-4

Cooking with Trader Joe's: Vegetarian
by Deana Gunn & Wona Miniati
ISBN 978-1-938706-01-1

Available everywhere books are sold.
Please visit us at

CookTJ.com